ESCAPE TO THE
Amalfi
COAST

Text and Photography by

Robert I. C. Fisher

Fodor's

FODOR'S TRAVEL PUBLICATIONS, INC.

NEW YORK • TORONTO • LONDON • SYDNEY • AUCKLAND • WWW.FODORS.COM

Special Sales

Fodor's Travel Publications are available at special discounts for bulk purchases for sales promotions or premiums. Special editions, including personalized covers, excerpts of existing guides, and corporate imprints, can be created in large quantities for special needs. For more information, contact your local bookseller or Special Markets, Fodor's Travel Publications, 201 E. 50th Street, New York, NY 10022. Inquiries from Canada should be directed to your local Canadian bookseller or sent to Random House of Canada, Ltd., Marketing Dept., 2775 Matheson Boulevard East, Mississauga, Ontario L4W 4P7. Inquiries from the United Kingdom should be sent to Fodor's Travel Publications, 20 Vauxhall Bridge Road, London, England SW1V 2SA.

PRINTED IN THE UNITED STATES OF AMERICA
10 9 8 7 6 5 4 3 2

Library of Congress Cataloging-in-Publication Data
Fisher, Robert I.C.
Escape to the Amalfi Coast / text and photography by Robert I.C. Fisher.—1st ed.
p. cm.
ISBN 0-679-00307-X (hardcover : alk. paper)
1. Amalfi Region (Italy)—Description and travel.   2. Sorrento Peninsula (Italy)—Description and travel.   I. Title.   II. Title: Amalfi
DG975.A42F57   1999
914.5'74—dc21   99-17700   CIP

Acknowledgments

The author owes much to many, particularly Arlene Wise, Brandy Whittingham, Thibaut de Toulouse-Lautrec (Capri), the Contessa Vallefiorita (Amalfi), Marta-Marie Lotti (for providing the wonderful wings of Alitalia), and—mamma mia!—Rosemary Biery. Finally, profusest thanks to Fabrizio La Rocca, for his wit, his style, and for the chance.

Credits

Creative Director and Series Editor: Fabrizio La Rocca
Editorial Director: Karen Cure
Art Director: Tigist Getachew

Editorial Production: Melissa Klurman
Production/Manufacturing: C.R. Bloodgood, Robert B. Shields
Map: David Lindroth

Most books on travel shelves are either long on the nitty-gritty and short on evocative photographs, or the other way around. We at Fodor's have aimed for a different balance in this slim volume, a book that's equal measure luscious magazine article and sensible, down-to-earth guidebook. Its pages, we hope, will inspire you as you plan your Amalfi Coast sojourn and guide you while you're on the road, to ensure that you have the best of all possible journeys.

We've combed every corner of the Amalfi Coast and the Bay of Naples in search of those quintessential places that embody the purest spirit of this miraculous coastline. It goes without saying that the roller-coaster ride down the legendary Amalfi Drive stood out among its pleasures. But there are many more: South of Naples, sparkling bays shelter lapis lazuli lagoons, and the sea melts into perpetually azure sky in ineffable vistas; anchored to the stair-stepped mountainsides are villas, gardens, convents dating from medieval times, and relics of once-omnipotent ancient Rome; fabled resorts and historic caravansaries are your shelter. And the views—those perfect views—are always with you.

Author and photographer Robert I. C. Fisher, while working to capture the magic of the coast, reports having fallen victim to its spell: During an ambrosial picnic at Ravello's Villa Cimbrone, where Greta Garbo once sought solitude, he felt suddenly enveloped in a cloud of perfume and heard a distinct swish of silk, as if the legendary screen goddess had just passed by. Was he dazed by the southern sun and the soft breezes so tangy with salt? Or was he simply bewitched by beauty?

It has been happening to travelers since the days of Odysseus and it will happen to you. So be prepared to embrace *il dolce far niente*—the sweetness of doing nothing. Forget your projects and deadlines. And escape to the Amalfi coast. You owe it to yourself.

—The Editors

IT ALL STARTED WITH CHANEL. WHEN THE GREAT COUTURIER PRONOUNCED suntans fashionable in the 1930s, trend setters in search of sun kissed sleepy fishing villages all across Italy into wakefulness. In Positano, the barefoot contessas and American playboys made their way to the Hotel Palazzo Murat, a baby Versailles built for an early 19th-century King of Naples a short walk from the shore, on one of the town's rare patches of flat land. Today you'll find Pergolesi concerts in its park, an enormous patio set with statues, waterfalls of bougainvillea (five kinds), and an air of easy elegance. You're at the center of town, at the base of an amphitheater of villas rising up all around. Still, you can barely see the shore, where it all began and where old Positano lingers—fishermen scowl at you if you get too close to their dinghies, moored a few steps away from the orderly

A Tale of Two Positanos

HOTELS LA FENICE AND PALAZZO MURAT

Positano is always charming, never more so that at the idyllic Hotel La Fenice, opposite, or the grand and glorious Palazzo Murat, above.

ranks of beach chairs. For a taste of the Positano that drew everyone here in the first place, head for the gently priced Hotel La Fenice, ranged up and down a cliff on the tranquil outskirts of town. Once the home of natives who lived close to the land, it is now, you may think, the most charming, most bewitching small hotel in the world. No matter that a million steps link your whitewashed cottage, smothered in bougainvillea, to the tiny crescent of cliff-crowded beach, far below. Rooms are simple but lovely with their folk crosses and shuttered windows opening onto the sea, and an elegant arbor-shaded stone terrace surrounds the sapphire pool. Owner Constantino Mandara still keeps chickens in the yard at the top; geese guard the iron gate at the bottom. Have a heart-to-heart with Mandara's mynah bird—he's fluent in English as well as Italian—and give three cheers for Chanel.

Positano's allure is most potent at Lo Guarracino—the most beautiful pizzeria in the world—or the Hotel La Fenice, left, or the Hotel Palazzo Murat, below.

Twilight arrives
in Positano—
swift, romantic,
with a touch of
sadness. The dome
of Santa Maria
Assunta looms
large when seen
from the main
beach
promenade.

THE SUN FAITHFULLY SHINES, SERENITY reigns, and just outside your hotel window in Ravello—the mountaintop town legendary for its solitude and romantic mystery—the Bay of Salerno is spread out like an inverted sky. Early morning's amber light glints on your breakfast tray and rouses songs from birds roosting in a nearby tree. Your own cozy roost is the Hotel Caruso Belvedere, a realm tended by the Caruso family, cousins to *the* Enrico. Although you might expect to hear an operatic overture, a monastic stillness prevails, broken only by the whispery sounds of sketchers sketching, poets poeticizing, writers writing. In fact, the hotel has long been sought out by the lions among literati: Graham Greene,

Inspiration's Realm

HOTEL CARUSO BELVEDERE, RAVELLO

Like Heaven upside down, the Bay of Salerno shimmers through the famous Gothic loggia at the Hotel Caruso Belvedere.

Gore Vidal, Tennessee Williams, and Virginia Woolf have all come here since Pantaleone Caruso opened the doors of the 14th-century Palazzo D'Afflitto as an inn. The pedigree reveals itself at every turn, from the Romanesque marble lions gracing the doorway to the spectacular Empire-era grand salon hung with the Caruso family's collection of 19th-century Neapolitan paintings. Just outside, gardens drape the hillside like tapestry, tempting you to meditate or put pen to paper. Later, take time out to head to the hotel dining room for lunch. Shaded by pretty red-and-white awnings and open to the bay, the setting could be from a Vincente Minelli movie, and, sure enough, from the church of San Giovanni del Toro across the road, here comes a wedding party—the bride all radiant smiles and fluttering white. Who wouldn't be inspired to poetry?

UNDER THE SORRENTO SUN, ORNATE VILLAS GLOW MAUVE, CHARTREUSE, AND pink, like a set for a Rossini opera; on the plaid ear-covers of the ponies pulling one-horse *carozze* around town, fuschia ball fringe bobs and nods with every step as policemen direct traffic with balletic grace. It's a happy scene, and it's no wonder that visitors come back year after year to nest, like migratory swallows, at the cafés on Piazza Tasso, closing their eyes dreamily when the waiters croon "Come Back to Sorrento." Nowhere is the town's considerable charm more potent than at the Albergo Lorelei et Londres. Just one step past its iron gate, the world seems younger by a century. With its facade colored a toasted terra cotta, its terrace planted with lemon trees and bougainvillea, and its balcony restaurant shaded by a vast awning, it's the

What Lucy Missed

ALBERGO LORELEI ET LONDRES, SORRENTO

Horse and carriage is the most suitable way to arrive at the Albergo Lorelei et Londres, Sorrento's most evocative 19th-century pensione.

very image of a turn-of-the-century pensione, like a stereopticon photo come to life—all that's missing are the tarantella dancers, petticoats and ribbons aswirl. Over your head, two rooftop signs weathered by a century of service proclaim "Londres" and "Lorelei," recalling an era when genteel English ladies vied with each other to secure "a room with a view." Lucy Honeychurch, E. M. Forster's impressionable heroine, would have loved Sorrento and this albergo, had she had the good fortune to sojourn here. Over *insalata caprese* on the relentlessly romantic terrace, with the entire Bay of Naples as dessert, you know you're the lucky one.

A Belle Epoque
treasure, Sorrento
is filled with lovely
views over the Bay
of Naples and
pretty palaces
such as the Palazzo
Correale.

WHIZZING CLOUDS PACE YOUR APPROACH INTO THE higher reaches of the Lattari mountains, the range that dominates the coast. Clumps of glossy myrtle and rosemary tickle your ankles. A sea of trees rises above you, while craggy volcanic cliffs tower in the distance, embodying flight and gravity simultaneously. You are tramping out from Montepertuso, the end of the line for the Positano bus, toward Nocelle, a hamlet attached like a wasp's nest to a mountainside 1,700 feet up. This trinket of a town is well known among Italy's serious hikers as the northern terminus of the Pathway of the Gods, the Sentiero degli Dei, the region's most challenging mountainside trail—although, as you learn, just getting to Nocelle is a test of mettle. Finally you catch a

La Dolce Vista

HIKING TO NOCELLE, NEAR POSITANO

glimpse of it, improbably pasted to the hillside. Before too long, it reveals itself fully: a stone alley, a scattering of houses and stairways, a minuscule piazza, a church, and Positano far below—a broader and higher vista than others along the coast, breathtaking in more ways than one. Meanwhile, sheep bleat, children giggle, and the rustling wind almost lulls you to sleep as you rest on the piazza's stone bench. Just as you stir yourself to wonder which way to turn to find the Sentiero degli Dei, a fresh-faced Madonna shouldering a baby appears with perfect timing and leads the way.

The path to Nocelle, high in the Lattari mountains, overlooks Positano,

THE SCENT OF PROFUMO DELLA TERRA, A blend of sun-warmed pinewood and pungent gentian, greets you at Punta Tragara, Capri's savage southern tip. Although lavish hotels and villas have somewhat defanged the terrain, it retains an elemental power. Nature's grandstanding is at its most awesome at the Grotta Matermania, the cavern where ancient Romans sacrificed to Cybele, the Earth Mother, every dawn; in the Cyclopean rock pinnacle called Pizzoluongo; and in the three rock masses known as the Faraglioni, which soar 300 feet above the water. Tines from Neptune's trident, you wonder? The royal fork, snapped off during an oceanic tantrum? Dramatically phallic, primordially geologic, the massive

Romancing the Stones

I FARAGLIONI AND PUNTA TRAGARA, CAPRI

Whether seen from a table at Il Canzone del Mare, poolside from Hotel Punta Tragara, or in a painting at the Hotel La Scalinatella, next page, the Faraglioni rocks remain Capri's top landmarks.

white marble Faraglioni draw couples by the score to the Tragara belvedere at sunset, when the stones blaze like hammered gold with the flashing of sun on the sea. Not far away, ingeniously stitched onto the cliffs, is the sculptural Hotel Punta Tragara, which the great architect Le Corbusier placed just so, to exploit the hypnotic power of the stone trio. Some guests never budge from their private balconies above the three rocks—they can't—except perhaps to drift down to the hotel's poolside restaurant, a dazzling study in indolence and wealth. Slip into a chair at one of the water's-edge tables, breathe in the jasmine-scented air and, maybe, adjust your pareo. Under the unwavering gaze of the Faraglioni, you've just gone native, Capri-style.

A BALCONY ON BEAUTY, THE TOWN OF SANT'AGATA SUI DUE GOLFI attracts two sets of pilgrims: one hungry for the stereoscopic panorama of the gulfs of Naples and Salerno (for which the community is named), the other seeking out the splendors of a table at Don Alfonso 1800, the only restaurant in southern Italy ever to win three Michelin stars. A meal here distills all that's most delicious under the Mediterranean sun, and the brilliance of chef Alphonso Iaccarino as he draws inspiration from his garden and from local culinary traditions make *la nuova cucina* newer still. The breaded lobster in *agrodolce* sweet-and-spicy glaze pays homage to the spice chest of Araby, brought to the Amalfi Republic by sea traders centuries ago. The canelloni alla sorrentina is a nod to the French Bourbons who ruled Naples in the 18th century—it's stuffed

Feasting Under the Sun

DON ALFONSO 1800, SANT'AGATA, NEAR SORRENTO

To accompany a meal at Campania's greatest restaurant, order a regal vintage from the wine cellar or have fun with a flambéed Vesuvio cocktail.

with asparagus, truffles, *and* foie gras. Lasagna napoletana is a revelation when made, as is everything here, of the very finest and freshest ingredients from the restaurant's own farm: elegant olive oils, lovingly tended tomatoes, snappingly fresh zucchini. The only pizza, a witty signature dessert, combines chocolate and genoise, with a sprinkling of confectioner's sugar standing in for the mozzarella. Great vintages from the famous cellar sited deep underneath the restaurant in an ancient king's tomb, appear regularly on the tables, but this evening, one group calls for a flaming Vesuvio cocktail, a trendy drink of the 20s and 30s that makes a fitting finale to a day in the looming presence of the mother of all volcanoes. This time, the drink neither erupts nor explodes into flames as it's meant to do, but no matter—the fireworks from chef Alfonso's kitchen are spectacular enough.

BLINK AND YOU MIGHT MISS CONCA DEI MARINI ON AN ENTRANCING CURVE of the Amalfi Coast. Some clever artist seems to have created the ideal of a coastal fishing village here, with all the requisite motifs: turquoise sea, weathered dories, bronzed fishermen, whitewashed cottages. But only part of the town is at the water's edge. As protection from the Moorish pirates who once roamed the coast, Conca was built up and down towering Monte San Pancrazio. On the shore, you can spot the villagers' first line of defense: a centuries-old Saracen tower, a square stone sentinel standing tall on a pile of rocks that lashes out into the sea like a scorpion's tail. Another marvel, Conca dei Marini's most celebrated, is the Emerald Grotto, a thicket of craggy stalactites and stalagmites that looks like a giant's set of Pick-Up-Sticks. Seeing any more of Conca requires

Between Sea & Sky

CONCA DEI MARINI, ALONG THE AMALFI COAST

With its wonderful patches of emerald set in a blue-glass lagoon, Conca dei Marini's harbor is one of the most enchanting visions of the Amalfi Coast.

you to scale Monte San Pancrazio via one of the rock-cut staircases that ribbon its face like so many vertical sidewalks. They provide the only route to four beautiful hillside churches set like base camps along the ascent to the village's summit. Near the first, San Pancrazio, a lone sheep appears—so nice to see a friendly face. An hour later, your stout shoes and stubborn pride finally deposit you at the 15th-century Convento di Santa Rosa, a massive gray monastery that looks as if it could have drifted over from Tibet. Take Via Roma across the cliff face and rest at the skyswimming church of Sant'Antonio, breathtakingly suspended over the azure sea. Don't linger too long—your cozy quarters at the seaview Hotel Belvedere await, with a restorative dinner. How you've earned them!

Crowds come to Conca to visit its famous seaside Emerald Grotto but often miss its mountaintop vistas, lofty convents, and the spectacular church of Sant'Antonio, hundreds of feet above the sea.

FOR NAPLES' DEVOUT AND LOTTERY-MAD CITIZENS THE REALLY BIG JACKPOT IS heavenly salvation, and little is left to chance in its pursuit. Amulets twinkle on skittish girls and their swains and on shawled duennas and friars right out of the Middle Ages—silver charms shaped like antelope horns, crescent moons, or hands with extended fingers, designed to warn away the pervasive evil eye, *la jettatura*. On the streets of Spaccanapoli, the old city's kaleidoscopic heart, azure-robed Madonnas sanctify local *salumerias*; armies of angelic cupids, clustered on marble spires called *guglie*, appeal for divine intervention; sublime church altarpieces inspire prayers; and in the crèche shops of Via San Gregorio Armeno, wise men, camel-borne ottomans, Holy Infants, angels, shepherds, beggars, and hunchbacks—some as small as a finger, others as bulky as a

Miracles & Treasures

SPACCANAPOLI, NAPLES

Gilded saints,
Baroque churches,
and crèche shops
make Spaccanapoli
the most colorful
neighborhood
in Naples.

boxer's forearm—keep the spirit of Christmas close all year long. In the district's churches, armies of gilded virgins kneel, waxwork saints suffer and bleed, and martyrs wear haloes of yellow neon. On September 19, one and all gather at the Duomo to celebrate the Miracle of the Liquefaction of the Blood of St. Gennaro; when the congealed sanguinary remains of the 4th-century saint are observed to liquefy in their silver and gold ampule, a white handkerchief is waved to the crowd and the annunciation is proclaimed to the TV cameras. "*Il miracolo!*" the cry goes up. But then, given Naples' history of plagues and cholera, the omnipresent menace of Vesuvius, the looming threat of earthquakes, *every* day in Naples is a miracle, as locals will tell you.

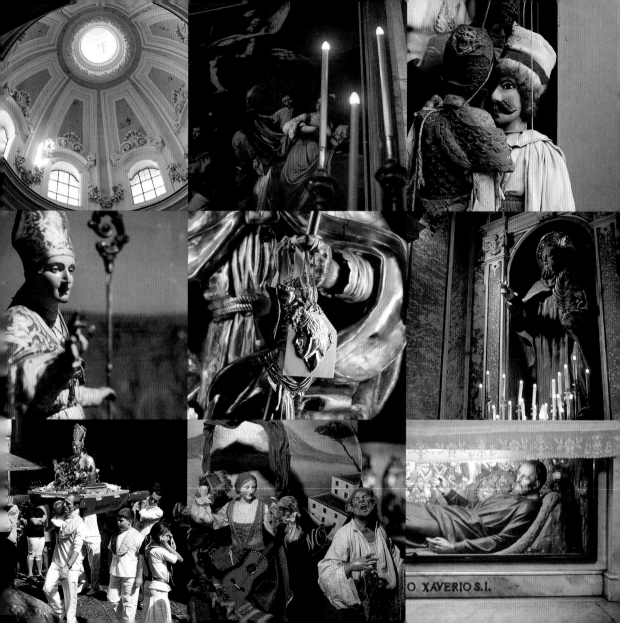

A VEIL OF CELESTIAL BLUE EXTENDS AS FAR AS YOU CAN SEE WHEN YOU stand on the upper terrace of the Villa Rufolo. The cerulean hue is not merely a color—it is a miracle, defining "blue" once and for all. It's no mystery why Landolfo Rufolo, described in Boccaccio's *Decameron* as one of Italy's richest men, chose this matchless mountain perch for the site of his 13th-century estate. A Scheherazadian extravaganza of Norman battlements and terraced gardens, with an Arab-Sicilian cloister, his villa was designed to welcome Moorish emirs and French kings. But it found its immortality centuries later when Richard Wagner unexpectedly arrived at its gates in February 1880 and stayed the night, banging out the second act of *Parsifal* on an untuned piano, accompanied only by his giant ego and a fierce thunderstorm. "Klingsor's gar-

The Bluest View in the World

VILLA RUFOLO, RAVELLO

den is found once again!" the great 19th-composer crowed of the wizard who ordered the seduction of the opera's saintly hero. Today Rufolo's medieval gardens, laid out by Pope Hadrian IV and still voluptuous with wisteria, scarlet sage, cyclamen, and bougainvillea, pay homage to Wagner's passionate spirit with an annual music festival; its midnight concerts, dawn serenades, and evening recitals are the stirring encore to the coast's flawless scenery.

The Villa Rufolo terrace overlooks
the entire Bay of Salerno, past
the Minori valley and Capo d'Orso
and on to the Cilento mountains.

From the Villa Rufolo to the Palazzo Sasso, opposite, Ravello sits upon a spur of Monte Cerreto, more than a thousand feet above the breathtaking bay.

THE MILLION-DOLLAR CONCEPT IS ROMANCE, UNAVOIDABLE IN VIEW OF THE setting: palatial stone terrace, mauve sky, a bay more mauve still, and, later, a canopy of stars and a calendar moon washing Mt.Vesuvius in silvery light. Even two left feet can't keep you from swaying to the beat of the orchestra as it plays (what else?) Cole Porter's "Night and Day." Preposterously beautiful, the Hotel Excelsior Vittoria is a gallant survivor of the Belle Epoque and a capsule of old Italy at its gabled and filigreed finest. In the Winter Garden, an intimate salon, lovers sip sherry, their glasses entwined, as a prelude to dinner in the Vittoria restaurant, an intoxicating study in gilt splendor and Art Nouveau charm. It is said that more marriage proposals are tendered here than in any other place in Italy, and no wonder—who could hold out in this Cinderella-ball

A Little Romance

HOTEL EXCELSIOR VITTORIA, SORRENTO

setting? For your own happily-ever-after moment, head for the seductive park, full of exuberant wisteria and roses whose fragrance revived many a spirit of an earlier time—Byron, Wilde, Verdi, emperors, kings. All came seeking inspiration, escape, dreams come true. You have only to look around to see that their Age of Romance is still with us. Only the cast of characters has changed.

Gigantic bouquets
grace the hotel's Vittoria
dining room, still Sorrento's
grandest restaurant.

ROUSSEAU'S SLEEPING GYPSY ONLY DREAMED OF PARADISE. THE HOTEL San Pietro is the real thing. Waving palm fronds keep the skyline in perpetual motion, grape arbors send out their tender vines to colonize walls and rafters, tawny odalisques in Armani swimsuits bask in the scorching sun, and roses, bougainvillea, dichondra, fuschia, and exotic orchids perfume the air. To all appearances growing organically out of the coastal rock, the hotel sprawls 300 feet above the sparkling Bay of Positano. A real cliffhanger of an address, it overlooks the spot where St. Peter's fishing boat first touched land in Italy. The lobby is filled with marble goddesses and gilded antiques, and the guest rooms are lavished with luxe, the faun-shaped faucets in their bathrooms dispensing *acqua* in wicked ways. At dawn, the hotel terrace stunningly flaunts

The Lush Life

HOTEL SAN PIETRO, POSITANO

the perfect view of Positano; at midday, a mirror-walled elevator deposits you on the private beach, where Mozzarella and Pomodoro, the bilingual resident macaws, fill in as gentleman hosts at a waterside bar. You can't help but wonder what Peter would have made of the place.

Positano at its most perfect:
the grand terrace of the
Hotel San Pietro, beautifully
adorned with majolica-tile
banquettes.

The Hotel San Pietro
offers great vistas
from guest-room
balconies as well as
from its grand
terrace, suspended
300 feet over the
shimmering bay.

LIKE A REMNANT OF AN ANCIENT GOLDEN AGE, THE VILLA POMPEIANA RECLINES luxuriantly along a cliff-top curve high above the Bay of Naples. Yet despite its classical lines and regal proportions, its pedestaled statues and marble urns, it is neither ancient nor a temple: A structure worthy of 19th-century painters Frederick Leighton and Alma-Tadema, it was built in 1905 for William Waldorf Astor on the site of the villa of Emperor Augustus' nephew, Agrippa Postumus. Today it is the elegant restaurant of the Bellevue Syrene, one of Sorrento's legendary hotels, a fantasia of ducal salons and Venetian chandeliers with a wistful, rustle-of-taffeta charm. In the villa, two jewel-like dining salons honor the features so beloved in the locale: the sun and the sea. In one room, the walls are the color of the Sorrento sun at its most Pompeian red; in the second, graceful

What Lord Astor Knew

VILLA POMPEIANA, SORRENTO

ESCAPE TO THE AMALFI COAST

Pompeian-style murals and a terrace fit for an emperor grace the Villa Pompeiana, Sorrento's most beautiful restaurant.

nymphs and sea creatures populate murals rimmed by trim of limpid blue. When in Sorrento, as in Rome, do the right thing: feast on Li Galli lobsters garnished with melon pearls; then have a dish of oranges in steeped Limoncello liqueur, all enjoyed on the restaurant's terrace under flickering iron torchères. Forests of columns frame an imperial panorama of the Bay of Naples that puts Vesuvius front and center, perennially cloud-swathed and always apparently just ready to erupt—a view that none other than Hermann Schliemann, discoverer of ancient Troy, called the finest in the land. Lord Astor certainly knew his real estate.

A sunset straight out of a postcard
seen from the Hotel Bellevue Syrene,
whose balconies and belvederes
rest on the most scenic curve of
the Bay of Naples.

ONCE UPON A TIME, WHEN RAVELLO RANKED AS THE QUIETEST TOWN IN THE world, Greta Garbo, the Aloof Goddess herself, showed up in the company of noted conductor Leopold Stokowski. After reporters promptly invaded the place, the pair fled their hotel to seek tranquil togetherness at the Villa Cimbrone, then a private home set 1,500 acrophobic feet above the sea. Built by England's Lord Grimthorpe (the horologist who designed the clockworks of London's Big Ben), this aerie is a turn-of-the-century fantasy complete with battlements and Wagnerian crypt, nestled within radiantly sunny gardens. Stroll down the so-called Allée of Immensity, past pergolas and rampageous roses, to the Belvedere of Infinity, a magnificent stone balcony that overlooks the Gulf of Salerno and, some say, a good part of the universe. Through the

Garbo's Shangri-la

VILLA CIMBRONE, RAVELLO

An ancient statue of the goddess Ceres greets visitors to the villa's Belvedere of Infinity, set 1,500 feet over the Gulf of Salerno.

softest mist, you see the sky above and the sea below. (Or is it the other way around? No matter: it is, as promised, infinity.) You'll have plenty of company at the belvedere, but a night at the villa, today one of Ravello's most ravishing hotels, is a peaceful antidote to the crush. Behind locked gates, you can steal away for a twilight picnic, then go for a last turn around the gardens, accompanied only by the spirits of the divine Greta and, ever the constant host, kindly Lord Grimthorpe himself.

The Belvedere of Infinity commands one of the most sublime prospects in the world: across the Gulf of Salerno all the way to the Cilento mountains and—your eyes do not deceive you—to the distant temples of Paestum.

The famous roses of Ravello color the villa's gardens, which are set with romantic lookouts, marble temples, and the 900-foot-long Allée of Immensity.

ON ALL WHO CROSS THE ARBORED THRESHOLD, THE CAPPUCCINI CONVENTO has a remarkable effect: It calms the heart, vanquishes anxiety, and encourages reflection and creativity. Perhaps the purifying factor is the remarkable altitude, high above Amalfi's harbor. Perhaps it's the mantra of the waves crashing on the distant shore. Or the residue of prayers sent off to heaven—not so far distant—beginning in the 13th century, when the structure was built as a convent. The friars stayed until the 19th century, when the building became a hostelry and a high point for Grand Tour travelers from Henry Wadsworth Longfellow to the Sitwells. For your own membership in their cloudhoppers club, simply step onto the skyhigh terrace. Or pace along the quarter-mile-long promenade, with Amalfi unfolding beneath you in a splen-

A World Apart

HOTEL CAPPUCCINI CONVENTO, AMALFI

Gazing at Amalfi from the hotel's legendary terrace may give you the "balustrade bend."

did panorama, then pull up a chair and let the sublime beauty of the place surround you. Later, wander along the hotel's hallways, infused with the spirit of seven centuries of peace, past Victorian lecterns and Renaissance chests, to your room. With its white walls, bureau, desk, and two pine beds, it consists only of essentials—as does your mind after a day or two in this tranquil place.

"Sweet the memory is to me/Of the land beyond the sea,/
Where the waves and mountains meet; Where amid her mulberry-trees/
Sits Amalfi in the heat,/Bathing ever her white feet/
In the tideless, summer seas . . . "

—Henry Wadsworth Longfellow, *Amalfi,* 1875

Like a white
acropolis, the
Cappuccini Convento
sits on a cliff above
Amalfi's harbor.
The plaque next to
the hotel entrance
honors Henry
Wadsworth
Longfellow.

another look at the sea, 500 vertigo-inducing feet below. It's a foregone con-clusion that you're in safe hands—that the Mario Andretti at the wheel knows every sneaky curve, every loose pebble, of the road. But as the bus revs up to juggernaut speed and you race through one hairpin curve so twisty that its front and back ends are visible at the same time, you note that both the driver and the young woman animatedly conversing with him seem oblivious to the sign over his head: *Non parlare all'autista* (Don't talk to the driver), and sheer fear makes every muscle tense. Eventually, though, you settle in and you soon fall under the spell of the splendid scenery that floats by: inviting villas, bluer-than-blue bays, patches of sheep, and Conca dei Marini's toy harbor, a lagoon

Blue Highway

THE AMALFI DRIVE

that's exactly the color of lapis lazuli in the sun. Then, before you can say "hyperventilate," the driver rounds the last curve of your spiral down to Amalfi. For him, ho-hum, it's all in a day's work. You and your fellow passen-gers swagger off the bus like heroes, and why not? It was a breathtaking run, and the amazing pictures you managed to snap are sure to be good for a laugh, and a few boasts, one day.

New and wonderful vistas open up every 100 yards along the Amalfi Drive—from the pastel houses of Il Furore to dizzying precipices that drop straight into the sea.

TINY IN SIZE, MERE GEOLOGICAL DOTS, THE THREE ISLANDS OFF THE COAST of Positano known as Li Galli are giants in the realm of legend. The tales of ancient Aegean mariners tell us that they are the petrified bodies of the Sirens, the long-haired sea deities—half mermaid, half woman—who tried to lure Odysseus and his crew with intoxicating songs onto their hazardous shoals. When the wily navigator lashed his men to the mast and sealed their ears, the story goes, the spiteful creatures chose to live out eternity as rocks, right here in the water four miles off Positano. To hear the Sirens' song at its most hypnotic, check into the Hotel Le Sirenuse, that celebrated pleasure palace run by the marquises Sersale, the family that once owned the whole archipelago; from almost any spot in the hotel, the petrified temptresses are

The Sirens' Call

LI GALLI ISLANDS, OFF POSITANO

Gennaro Capraro makes a personable guide to La Castellucia. The prettiest view of the Sirens' island home is from Hotel Le Sirenuse.

in plain view. Or call on Positano's Pavarotti-sized Gennaro Capraro to ferry you out to the islands from the town harbor. At La Castellucia, the center islet, huge rocks stand guard over sandy shores, shards of classical amphorae glint in the sun, and you can still make out traces of eroded anchorages, relics of ancient Roman times. Gennaro fills you in on the rest of the story, up to this century, when La Castellucia's square Saracen tower was the vacation retreat of those masters of the ballet universe, Leonide Massine and Rudolf Nureyev. Anchor alongside the other two islands, Gallo Lungo and La Rotunda, for a dip into the translucent waters, and you will morph into a sea creature yourself. After some hours, and perhaps a few glasses of wine, a sense of narcosis sets in: The Sirens are irresistible, even today.

Don't miss the entrancing views over Positano and the Li Galli islands from the terraces of the Hotel Le Sirenuse.

OVER THE YEARS, CAPRI FEVER HAS STRUCK ARTISTS, POETS, BEACHCOMBERS, and billionaires. Under the island's spell, some became permanent residents, and monumentalized their passion in the lavish villas that now litter the island's hillsides. The most extraordinary exile was Sweden's Dr. Axel Munthe, who ministered first to kings and emperors and later tended victims of plague and cholera in the worst slums of Naples. When he arrived in Capri in 1896 he had planned only a casual visit, but succumbing to the island's charms, he found himself a hilly perch—an abandoned chapel—and never left. Dark tales clung to the spot, once the site of the villa of Emperor Tiberius, best known for his role in sentencing a certain carpenter from Galilee. The ringing of bells, missing from the chapel, was said to be the spirit of Emperor Tiberius begging forgiveness. Munthe ban-

Wish Fulfillment

VILLA SAN MICHELE, ANACAPRI

ished the shadows, making his villa the queen of Capri's houses as he fitted it out with Gothic furniture and a wealth of antiquities, restoring the chapel, adding a terrazzo-floored atrium and a garden just this side of fable. Here, mossy pathways lined with plump piñatas of flowers lead to a grand colonnade with a panorama of the entire Bay of Naples. Before you leave, be sure to visit the villa's famous stone sphinx, which reclines in its own belvedere at the end of the colonnade. Stroke its hind legs with your left hand and hope for your heart's desire: Legend has it that your wish will come true.

Among the wonders of
the Villa San Michele
are a Roman-style
loggia set with antique
busts and the
Terrace of the Sphinx,
which overlooks the
Bay of Naples.

FOOD IS NEXT TO GODLINESS IN AMALFI—NEVER MORE SO THAN AT THE Hotel Luna Convento, a former convent founded in 1222 by St. Francis of Assisi and now the setting for one of Italy's famed cooking schools. Lessons are in a round stone tower that's so close to the water it seems to float. On this lovely June day, six pairs of eyes grow teary with rapture (or is it the chopped onion?) in the prep work for the day's recipe: seabass poached in *acqua pazza*, or "crazy water"—actually, seawater spiked with garlic, tomatoes, and herbs. "Remember," chef Enrico Franzese says, proudly pulling a plump fish from the frigid depths of his refrigerator, his eyes twinkling in appreciation of the apparent contradiction: "The uglier the fish, the tastier the dish." Franzese is a native Amalfitano, the real McCoy, steeped in generations of

Crazy Water, Sweet Lemons

HOTEL LUNA CONVENTO COOKING SCHOOL, AMALFI

Chef Enrico Franzese is a charmer extraordinaire. His signature dishes start with clams and *boccadoro* (sea bass).

local culinary tradition. He considers his family recipes a priceless inheritance, and confides that some of his simpler, now classic, preparations were once reserved especially for Sundays, when whole families would gather over lasagna Sorrentina after hours of fasting and prayer. During the week, pasta-making is leavened with field trips around Amalfi: a market tour, for instance, or a walk to the groves of the nearby Valle dei Mulini, where the trees are heavy with *sfusati*, the native lemons whose unusually sweet flavor is perfect for pastries. Tomorrow, it's back to the kitchen to master lemon profiteroles— delicious! After one never-to-be-forgotten taste, you'll sprinkle a little confectioner's sugar over your shoulder and count your blessings.

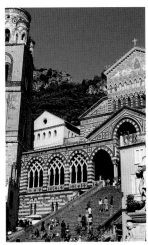

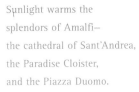

Sunlight warms the
splendors of Amalfi—
the cathedral of Sant'Andrea,
the Paradise Cloister,
and the Piazza Duomo.

YOU LEARNED ANCIENT HISTORY AT CECIL B. DEMILLE'S KNEE, IN FILM EPICS that regaled us with extravagant detail: awesome expanses of pristine marble, ethereally billowing silk, staircases as wide as a palace, a cast of thousands in costumes heavy with gold. You won't find such splendor at Pompeii, entombed mid-breath when Vesuvius erupted in 79 AD, but just one railway stop away is a site worthy of every lingering MGM fantasy: the excavated town of Oplontis and, within it, the still-fabulous villa of Nero's amber-tressed empress, Poppaea Sabina, notorious for her addiction to opulence. Here, near pools once stocked with jewel-collared carp, ancient murals burn in vivid color. In a splendid faux colonnade, alabaster trompe l'oeil columns support walls slathered with Pompeian vermilion and topped with gilding. Painted masks,

At Home with an Empress

VILLA POPPAEA, OPLONTIS, TORRE ANNUNZIATA

Even the greatest houses in nearby Pompeii cannot compare with the ancient splendor of the Villa Poppaea

frozen in theatrical grimaces, express the shock of tragedy; peacocks strut in true-to-life dazzle; floor-to-ceiling sections of scenery create illusions of the moment. All were created for the pleasure of Nero, then scandalizing Rome by acting on the public stage (to great acclaim, of course) and soon to torch the city as a riff, to add credibility to his performance of *The Sack of Troy*. All the world was a stage for Poppaea, too, and it's easy to imagine her dramatic entry into these salons: her breast heaving under a weight of rubies and emeralds, her plump hand summoning trays of truffled flamingo. Destiny, ever the sly intruder, put an end to all that when Vesuvius gave Oplontis a taste of lava, only enough to preserve it for posterity. That was just right, say the spirits keeping vigil over its treasured remains.

A HALF HOUR'S WALK FROM THE CENTER OF Sorrento, in the hamlet of Sant'Agnello, you will come to a grand-ducal iron gate, guarded by a Swiss cottage of a gatehouse. Pass through it and follow the snaking carriageway through the dim, cool tunnel of greenery. Suddenly you debouch, like Alice flying out of the rabbit hole, into the sun-dappled Parco dei Principi. This hidden wonder, a patch of artfully designed woodlands and meandering footpaths, was built in 1792 as the setting for a villa by Count Leopoldo of Siracusa, cousin to the royal Bourbons. Here, the count and a young Russian noblewoman named Tania, the love of his life, collected Capodimonte porcelain and languished on velvet sofas, teasing lapdogs, until Tania's sudden death one

The Secret Garden

THE PARCO DEI PRINCIPI, SANT'AGNELLO, NEAR SORRENTO

Built around the Count of Siracusa's villa, the Parco dei Principi, opposite, is just one gate down the road from the Grand Hotel Cocumella's 16th-century chapel, above.

Easter week shattered the idyll and the count went mad with grief. Today, a Temple of Love and diminutive Bridge of Love—inscribed with a poem by Désireé, Napoleon's first amour, who came here often—recall the romance. Take a stroll down the single long allée of perfectly tonsured Washingtonia palms, circle the mounds of golden African poppies and wander along the deeply shaded, bloom-fragranced pathways through this genteel wilderness; Sorrento is a million miles—and a century—away. On summer evenings couples still banter and flirt in the count's gardens, now part of the Hotel Parco dei Principi; attend Vivaldi concerts at the private chapel in the adjacent Cocumella gardens; and— with a vista of the Bay of Naples as their witness—pledge undying devotion with a passion that foresees only happy endings.

The Temple of Love is one
nook in the Parco dei Principi.
Right and top, the gardens of
the Grand Hotel Cocumella
overlook the villas of Sant'Agnello,
Vesuvius, and the Bay of Naples.

All the Details

A M A L F I *(9F)*

Amalfi, nestled between the green Valle dei Mulini and the blue Gulf of Salerno, is that rarity of rarities: a truly picturesque city. Threaded with rambling passages and covered staircases that suggest the Oriental caravansary of romance, the city is most famous for its medieval cathedral, which stands as glittering testament to the city's reign as a great maritime republic from the 9th to 11th centuries, when it rivaled Pisa, Genoa, and Venice. Amalfi is the tourist hub for the Amalfi Coast, so the peace and quiet it has so long traded on can be ruined by convoys of tours buses and a tangle of cameras and elbows. If you know where to look, however, you can still immerse yourself in the city's time-burnished splendor.

DISTANCES 38 miles southeast of Naples, 20 miles west of Salerno, 11 miles southeast of Positano.

GETTING THERE Amalfi is the terminus for SITA's major coastal bus routes, so there are frequent departures and arrivals at the harborfront on Piazza Flavio Gioia. The main route along the Amalfi Drive serves many small towns along the coast. An express bus between Naples and Amalfi follows a thrilling route high into the Lattari mountains (5-9E-G) and takes about 2 hours.

WHEN TO GO Protected from northerly winds by the Lattari mountains, Amalfi enjoys temperate weather year-round. Because the city faces the southern sun, you can swim from April to December. Summer brings a full slate of cultural events, including the Notte concerts on Piazza Duomo. The festival of Sant'Andrea runs from June 25 to 30. It climaxes with the oft-photographed run of the saint's reliquary bust, atop the shoulders of 10 men, up the steep cathedral steps. Good Friday sees a spectacular candlelit procession through the darkened streets. In 2000 and every fourth year thereafter, Amalfi holds the historic regatta of the ancient four Sea Republics on the first Sunday in June (Genoa, Pisa, and Venice host in other years).

WHAT TO SEE Forming the centerpiece of Amalfi's **Piazza del Duomo** is the stirring 11th-century cathedral of **Sant'Andrea**. Set atop a flight of 62 steps, with a campanile resembling a minaret, a porch covered in Byzantine-style mosaics, an Arab-Norman cloister dating from 1268, and bronze doors cast in Constantinople, the cathedral testifies to the wealth of Amalfi while its trade flourished with Tunis, Tripoli, Algiers, and points east. The piazza, set with cafés and a fountain, is the heart of the city and the natural starting point for a tour. Go one block to the

waterfront and the **Piazza Flavio Gioia**, then turn left and walk up the Corso delle Repubbliche Marinare to the **Hotel Luna Convento**, at the top of the hill. After visiting its medieval cloister, head back to town along the harbor, then return to the Piazza del Duomo to pick up the charming Via Annunziata, a pedestrian path that traces an ascending cliff-side trail past Amalfi's prettiest pastel houses to the **Hotel Cappuccini Convento**. Have lunch on the famous veranda, then return to town and follow Via Genova and Via Capuano to the **Valle dei Mulini**, the picturesque valley dotted with the town's historic paper mills.

LODGING OPTIONS

Albergo S. Andrea: This 12-room budget charmer is on the main square in a historic palazzo opposite Amalfi's cathedral. Piazza Duomo, 84011 Amalfi (SA), tel. 089/871023. Doubles 95,000 lire.
Hotel Santa Caterina: When Elizabeth Taylor and Richard Burton camped out in Amalfi in 1962, they chose this legendary, luxurious resort. Its centerpiece, a turn-of-the-century mansion, is on a terraced hillside above the sea, surrounded by lush gardens that are anchored by three villa annexes, one a Victorian chalet. A private elevator takes you down to the spectacular beach and pool area, where a waterside restaurant offers some of the best cuisine in Amalfi. There are 54 rooms, 9 suites, and 3 villas. Strada Amalfitana 9, 84022 Amalfi (SA), tel. 089/871012, fax 089/871351, www.starnet.it/santacaterina. Doubles 590,000 lire, suites and villas 1,200,000 lire.

FOR DETAILS For bus information, call 089/871009. Amalfi's tourist information center is at Corso delle Repubbliche Marinare (tel. 089/871107).

HOTEL CAPPUCCINI CONVENTO

A World Apart, p. 58

Since being transformed from a convent in 1821, the Cappuccini Convento has often been called southern Italy's most beautiful hotel. Its panoramic veranda so moved Henry Wadsworth Longfellow that he composed a poem to honor the spot, and even Richard Wagner was inspired to forsake his room to camp out under the stars. Lunch on the veranda is the high point, literally and figuratively, of any trip to the Amalfi Coast. There are 48 rooms and 6 suites.

BASICS Via Annunziatella 46, 84011 Amalfi (SA), tel. 089/871877, fax 089/871886, www.amalfinet.it/cappuccini. Doubles 260,000—300,000 lire, suites 400,000 lire.

HOTEL LUNA CONVENTO COOKING SCHOOL

Crazy Water, Sweet Lemons, p. 72

Built around a cloister founded by St. Francis of Assisi, the Luna Convento was the first hotel to open on the Amalfi Coast, in the 19th century, and since then has welcomed everyone from Henrik Ibsen to Ingrid Bergman. Perched on a rocky promontory on the Gulf of Salerno, the complex includes 46 rooms and suites, a Baroque church, a bay-side swimming pool, and the Saracen tower where chef Enrico Franzese hosts weeklong cooking seminars. The chef speaks only Italian, but Rosemary Anastasio, an English-born Amalfi resident, serves as a gracious interpreter and guide for the mostly American students. Southern Italian cooking is the focus; classes are held every morning, followed by sightseeing excursions around Amalfi and farther afield to **Pompeii** (7D), **Sorrento** (5F), and **Ravello** (9F), with a special trip to Ristorante Don Alfonso 1800.

BASICS Via Pantaleone Comite 19, 84001 Amalfi (SA), tel. 089/871002, fax 089/871333, www.amalficoast.it.hotelluna; U.S. reservations from Judy Ebrey, Cuisine International, Box 25228, Dallas, TX 75225, tel. 214/373—1161, fax 214/373—1162, www.lglobal.net/cuisineint. Program cost, including room and board, $2,400—$2,700 per student; doubles without program 300,000 lire, suites 450,000 lire.

ALONG THE AMALFI COAST

State Highway 163 between the Sorrentine Peninsula and Salerno, better known to Americans as the Amalfi Drive and to Italians as the Via Smeraldo (Emerald Road) and the Nastro Azzuro (Blue Ribbon), is one of the most breathtaking coastal drives known to man, rewarding visitors with views that are the equal of any in creation, with panoramas unfolding at every turn.

THE AMALFI DRIVE

Blue Highway, p. 64

To make this trip it's a good idea to forsake your car for a bus: You won't have to focus on the traffic, and from the elevation of a bus seat you will get a better look at the scenery over the high stone barrier that keeps errant drivers on the straight and narrow. It doesn't matter if you travel from west to east (from Sorrento to Amalfi, which is what most people do) or vice versa. The key for the best views is to sit on the sea side of the bus—that is, on your left as you board the bus if you're starting in Sorrento, on your right if you begin in Amalfi. The trip between Sorrento (5F) and Amalfi (9F) generally takes an hour and 20 minutes. You'll pass through **Sant'Agnello** (5F), **Piano di**

Sorrento (6F), **Meta** (6F), **Positano** (7F) (the bus stops at Chiesa Nuova in the upper town), Positano (the second stop is called Sponda, and it's in the lower town), **Praiano** (8G), and **Conca dei Marini** (8F); along the way the bus passes through many other coastal towns, including **Furore** and **Vettica Maggiore**.

Tickets must be purchased in advance (remember to time-stamp your ticket in the machine at the front of the bus as you board because conductors often make spot checks). You'll find ticket vendors in cafés, bars, and newsstands area-wide; the Sorrento train-station newsstand is where most people stock up, but between noon and 4 PM, when it's closed, head for the cafés on the square two blocks to the south. Note that if you want to get off anywhere along the road, whether at a hotel or at one of the villages en route, alert the bus driver when boarding.

BASICS SITA buses make the trip along the coast 22 times daily between 6:30 AM and 10 PM. Wallet-size SITA bus schedules are available at ticket vendors, regional tourist offices, and from hotel concierges. Or contact SITA in Naples, at 081/593–4644.

CONCA DEI MARINI (8F)

Between Sea & Sky, p. 28

Conca dei Marini, 3 miles west of Amalfi, feels much farther than that from the madding crowd. One of the coast's most tranquil alternatives to crowded Positano and Amalfi, the town has long been favored by the international set—Jacqueline Kennedy, Carlo Ponti, and the Agnelli and Chandon families have all summered here. Walk in any direction from the SITA bus stop (in front of the Hotel Belvedere), and you'll find impressive sights. To the west the **Capo di Conca** promontory, along the main highway in the direction of Positano, is the site of a lido and restaurant nestled under a 16th-century Saracen tower. From there it's just 15 minutes on foot to the famous **Grotta dello Smeraldo (Emerald Grotto)** (8G). To the east of the bus stop, along the main highway, there are fine harbor views. South of the SITA bus stop, to the left of the Hotel Belvedere as you face the water, a staircase leads to the tiny **harbor** (unfortunately, a major landslide in 1997 closed its beach and café and the **chapel of Santa Maria della Neve** for the foreseeable future). From the Belvedere it's about an hour on foot to the northern reaches of town and Conca's beautiful churches. To get there, look for the staircase opposite the hotel and head upward, along the steep roads and *salite* (staircases). Halfway up you'll come to the town's tiny piazza, which has a café. To the east of the piazza follow the road for a half mile to the 16th-century **Convento di Santa Rosa** (now a private home). A half mile west of the piazza along Via 2 Maggio and Via Roma is the spectacularly sited church of **Sant'Antonio da Padova**. If you want to spend more time hiking in Conca dei Marini and the surrounding hills, see Julian Tippet's trail guide, *Landscapes of Sorrento and the Amalfi Coast* (Sunflower Press,

London, 1996), available at many newsstands along the coast.

BASICS Grotta dello Smeraldo: Apr.—Sept., daily 9—5; Oct.—Mar., daily 10—4. Admission 5,000 lire.

LODGING OPTIONS

Hotel Belvedere: Decade after decade, guests return to this 35-room hotel, whose core is a turn-of-the-century villa, and every year they are delighted to find it unchanged. Long presided over by the Lucibello family, it is on a hillside above the sea and is popular among German and English travelers, who spend entire days floating in the swimming pool, hundreds of feet below the hotel, at water's edge. (One of life's perfect moments: watching from the pool as your drink order is sent up to the hotel bar in a wicker basket on a pulley.) The old-fashion hotel lobby is overfilled with armchairs; guest rooms are uncluttered and are cooled by balconies shaded with apricot-hued awnings. Via Smeraldo, 84010 Conca dei Marini (SA), tel. 089/831282, fax 089/831439. Doubles 180,000—240,000 lire, suites 260,000—320,000 lire. **Hotel Le Terrazze:** All of the 35 rooms in this modern, spanking clean establishment near the Hotel Belvedere have balconies with views of Conca's spectacular seaside villas. Via Smeraldo, 84010 Conca dei Marini (SA), tel. 089/831290, fax 089/831296. Doubles 180,000 lire.

CAPRI (2-3H)

Since the age of the Roman emperors, travelers have flocked to the Bay of Naples's most beautiful island to see its mysterious grottoes, sapphire bays, peerless vistas, and spectacular ruins. That means crowds, especially in July and August. So discriminating travelers forsake Capri town and famous sights like the Blue Grotto and seek out private villas, secluded hotels, and off-the-beaten-track locales such as the Punta Tragara, with its vista of the famous I Faraglioni, and make the 10-minute trip by bus to the village of Anacapri (Upper Capri), where the Villa San Michele, a former private home in a ravishing setting, is open to the public as a museum.

DISTANCES The isle of Capri is 12 miles southeast of Naples, 5 miles east of Sorrento.

GETTING THERE Capri is easily reached by *aliscafi* (hydrofoil) in about 45 minutes and, less expensively, via the regular ferry, which takes one and a half hours. Both depart from the Molo Beverello in Naples and the Marina Piccola in Sorrento; boats dock in Capri at the Marina Grande, from which you can travel to Capri via funicular (by bus off-season).

WHEN TO GO Capri is sunny and balmy as early as April and as late as October, so you don't miss anything by skipping busy July and August. There are cultural events from April through December. Religious festivals highlight June and September: the Feast of San Antonio in Anacapri on June 13, the feast at the church of Santa Maria del Soccorso on Monte Tiberio on September 7, and the procession of Santa Maria alla Libera at the Marina Grande on September 13. Many Italians visit Capri on New Year's Eve, and islanders stir from their wintry pace to welcome hordes of merrymakers for days-long celebrations.

FOR DETAILS Tourist offices are in Capri town under the clock on the Piazza Umberto I (tel. 081/837−0686), in Anacapri at Via Orlandi 19A (tel. 081/837−1524), and on the pier at Marina Grande (tel. 081/837−0634). Also check out Capri's Web site, www.caprinet.it.

I FARAGLIONI AND PUNTA TRAGARA (3H)

Romancing the Stones, p. 22

Stroll a half hour from Capri's main piazzetta and you'll come to one of the island's most spectacular areas—the **Località Faraglioni**, named for the three rocky spires that anchor the southeast coast. To get there, take Via V. Emanuele and Via Camerelle from the piazzetta; tree-shaded Via Tragara, full of 19th-century villas and gardens, will take you to Capri's famed vantage point, the **Punta Tragara**, where two diverging **paths** beckon. One follows the southeast cliff face of the island: with its hundreds of steps, this path is more enjoyable when you start this path instead at the **Arco Naturale (Natural Arch)**, the island's unique stone archway carved by geologic erosion. The other path was a favorite of poet Pablo Neruda, who lived on the island in the 1950s and whose poetry is emblazoned on a plaque at the trailhead. Some visitors skip the walk, which involves 187 steps down the mountainside to the base of I Faraglioni, and catch a bus at the piazzetta for the **Marina Piccola**, where they charter boats for the 10-minute trip to the rocks. At the base of **La Stella**, the one rock that is attached to land, is the Ristorante Da Luigi, where the menu comes with a beach mattress. Have a bite and let yourself be mesmerized by the view.

The best way to explore the Località Faraglioni is to hike along the **Giro dell'Arco Naturale**, one of Capri's most scenic cliff-side trails. To get there from Capri's main piazzetta, follow either Via Longano or Via Le Botteghe to the end of Via Matermania, where you'll find the arbor-covered Ristorante Le Grotelle and the trail. Fueled with savory pizza you can either hike toward the Arco Naturale, about 10 minutes away, or head in the other direction down to the **Grotto di Matermania**, a natural cave used by ancient Romans as a shrine honoring the Mater Magna. After you've trekked what seems like hundreds of steps from the restaurant, the path levels out near the **Punta Massulo** and the **Villa Malaparte**, a monument of modernist design built in 1932 by Adelbergo Libera, on its own promontory. The trail next leads past the **Villa Solitaria**—Capri's most evocative turn-of-the-century house, perched above the sea—and the **Pizzoluongo**, a stone pinnacle. The three Faraglioni soon loom ahead. Count on an hour to do the entire trail. You can emerge from the wooded trail at the Punta Tragara viewpoint. From there the Via Tragara leads back to Capri town.

BASICS Ristorante Da Luigi: Via Faraglioni 2, tel. 081/837−0951. Ristorante Le Grotelle: Località Arco Naturale, tel. 081/837−5719.

VILLA SAN MICHELE (2H)

Wish Fulfillment, p. 70

A 10-minute walk up the Via Capodimonte from Anacapri's **Piazza Monumento** brings you to the foot of **Monte Solaro**, once the site of one of Emperor Tiberius's 12 imperial Capri villas and now the location of Villa San Michele, built in the late 19th century. After Dr. Axel Munthe bought the land in 1896 he incorporated excavated antiquities into the villa he built on the spot. The rooms are filled with medieval choir stalls, inlaid Byzantine tables, marble busts, and antique statues (even J. Pierpont Morgan, with his millions, couldn't persuade Munthe to sell one of them). Beyond the sculpture loggia is the villa's famous **pergola**, covered with roses, honeysuckle, and wisteria, with a **view** to the distant shores of Calabria. At the far end is the **belvedere** with the famous sphinx and the tiny **chapel** dedicated to San Michele Archangelo, for whom the villa was named. Munthe—who found fame as physician to kings and emperors and later made a fortune as author of the best-selling *The Story of San Michele* (1929)—had prodigious compassion: he ministered to the poor of Naples and Capri and bought land around his lofty villa to create a bird sanctuary. Today the Fondazione Axel Munthe offers **hikes** through the preserve to the ruined castle of Barbarossa, as well as Friday-night **concerts** in summer.

BASICS Via Capodimonte 34, tel. 081/837−1401. Daily May−Sept. 9−6; Mar.−Apr. and Oct. 9:30−4:30; Nov.−Feb. 10:30−3:30. Admission 6,000 lire.

LODGING OPTIONS

Hotel Punta Tragara: Crowning a rocky point over the sea, this wondrously beautiful hotel—which Le Corbusier designed as a private home in the 1940s and which later became a favored retreat of dignitaries such as Churchill and Eisenhower—has the best view in Capri, directly above I Faraglioni. It's no less than palatial, with its travertine marble lobby, baronial fireplaces, and 47 antique-bedecked rooms and suites (each with a panoramic balcony). The bougainvillea-lavished gardens are the matchless setting for two seawater pools and La Bussola, perhaps the prettiest restaurant in Campania. Via Tragara 57, 80073 Capri (SA), tel. 081/837−0844, fax 091/837−7790. Doubles 280,000−350,000 lire, suites 380,000−520,000 lire. Closed Nov.−

Easter. **Hotel Villa Certosa:** A stone's throw from Capri's most historic monastery, this 20-room hotel is delightfully homey, with a lovely palm-shaded terrace. Via Certosa 3/B, 80073 Capri (SA), tel. and fax 081/837−0005. Doubles 170,000−240,000 lire. Closed Nov.−Mar. **La Scalinatella:** Inspired by the historic Villa Morocco next door, Capri's most chic hotel is a whitewashed Moorish fantasy of arabesque windows, white linen sofas, Empire-style antiques, and Chinese porcelain figures; the poolside environment is as stylish as the sun worshippers who populate it. Balconies of the 22 rooms and 8 suites have dreamy views of Capri town. Via Tragara 8, 80073 Capri (SA), tel. 081/837−0633, fax 081/837−8291. Doubles 590,000−730,000 lire, suites 750,000−850,000 lire. Closed Nov.−Mar. **Villa Helios:** Occupying one of Capri's Art Nouveau villas, this guest house with 15 simply furnished rooms is run by the local Diocesi of San Stefano. A chapel occupies the ground floor, and a lovely terrace over-looks the villa's extensive orchards. Via Croce 4, 80073 Capri (SA), tel. and fax 081/837−0240. Doubles 150,000 lire. No credit cards. Closed Nov.−Apr.

N A P L E S *(3A-B)*

Campania, which encompasses the Amalfi Coast, the island of Capri, and the Sorrento promontory, has more beautiful sights than may be fair for any single region to possess. So it may be only fitting that it also includes the city of Naples, one of Europe's noisiest, most chaotic centers. Nonetheless, this city in the shadow of Vesuvius is a treasure with myriad facets. Many sights stand out: the Castel Nuovo, the Museo di Capodimonte, the Aquarium, and the famed archaeological museum. Then there are the Neapolitans themselves. You have only to listen to them talk—or watch them—to be charmed by their gaiety and undiluted spontaneity. The best place to do this is in Spaccanapoli, the relentlessly picturesque neighborhood smack in the center of town between Via Toledo and Via Duomo; the area takes its name (which translates as "Split Naples") from its main street, which cuts the historic center in half.

DISTANCES 136 miles southeast of Rome, 38 miles southeast of Amalfi.

GETTING THERE Arriving by bus (often from Naples's Aeroporto Capodichino) or by train, most travelers stop first in the Piazza Garibaldi, hub for many bus lines and site of the Stazione Centrale.

WHEN TO GO Naples celebrates the Miracle of the Blood of San Gennaro every September 19 at the Duomo, beginning at 9AM. By noon, the blood of the saint—martyred in the 3rd century AD by the

emperor Diocletian—usually liquefies in its silver ampule before rapt thousands. September 18 is marked by a ceremonial cortege (from the Piazza del Carmine to the Piazza del Duomo) and other joyful cel-ebrations. The Miracle is also celebrated on the first Saturday in May (when the relics are paraded to the Chiesa di Santa Chiara) and on December 16, the anniversary of the threatened eruption of Vesuvius in 1631.

FOR DETAILS The Stazione Centrale has an office of the Ente Provinciale per il Turismo (tel. 081/268779); other tourist offices are in the Palazzo Reale, Piazza del Plebiscito (081/418744), and at the Piazza del Gesù Nuovo 7 (tel. 081/5523328), in the center of Spaccanapoli. For San Gennaro details, contact the Comitato Diocesano S. Gennaro (tel. 081/446103).

SPACCANAPOLI (3B)
Miracles & Treasures, p. 32

Along Spaccanapoli, the street that slices through the heart of historic Naples, once-grand palazzi and 19th-century tenements towering over the pavement create dim urban canyons; overhead, laundry flut-ters in the sun, and everywhere there are beautiful Baroque churches, Renaissance palaces, and Rococo cloisters. The city's first golden age was during the reigns of Charles and Robert of Anjou, who built churches that are monuments of 14th-century Angevin Gothic. During the 17th century the Baroque style came to the fore under new Spanish rulers; the Neapolitan take—characterized by gilded stucco work, carved spirals, and a profusion of ornament—found its apogee in the largest church of the district, the **Gesù Nuovo**. During Bourbon rule in the 18th century, Baroque gave way to Rococo; the best exam-ples are the **Cappella Sansevero**, the church of **San Gregorio Armeno**, and the **Chiostro delle Clarisse**, the exquisite majolica-tiled cloister of **Santa Chiara**.

In Spaccanapoli, strangers quickly become participants: come pre-pared to enjoy yourself. A good walk starts at the district's official gateway, the **Piazza del Gesù Nuovo**, several blocks west of Via Toledo, one of Naples's main avenues and bus routes. Landmarked by the **Guglia dell'Immacolata**—a towering statue-covered marble spire erected in 1743 to honor the Virgin—the piazza is the site of the sumptuous Baroque church of the Gesù Nuovo, built by the Jesuits in 1584, as well as the severe Gothic church of Santa Chiara, built by Robert of Anjou in the 14th century. Santa Chiara is home to the qui-etest spot in noisy Spaccanapoli: the celebrated cloisters of the Chiostro delle Clarisse, transformed in 1742 into a Rococo-era show-piece with colorful majolica-tile overlay on its columns and benches. Off the piazza outside Santa Chiara is the pedestrian-only Spaccanapoli, laid out by the ancient Romans. Turning to the right onto Spacca outside Santa Chiara you pass several palazzi and come to the beautiful **Piazza San Domenico**, framed by the **Guglia di San**

Domenico (1737) and the apse of **San Domenico Maggiore**. In spring and summer, district residents make this piazza their living room—the umbrella tables are courtesy of **Scaturchio**, Naples's celebrated gelateria. Head up the right side of the piazza to Via Francesco de Santis and the **Cappella Sansevero** (1590), the tomb-chapel of the Sangro di San Severo family (open Monday and Wednesday—Saturday 10–5, Tuesday and Sunday 10–1). Designed by Prince Raimondo di Sangro, notorious alchemist and occultist, the chapel contains three extraordinarily theatrical 18th-century sculptures, including Giuseppe Sanmartino's *Veiled Christ*. Backtrack to the Largo Corpo di Napoli on the Spaccanapoli roadway and the pretty 18th-century church of **Sant'Angelo a Nilo**, with the statue of the Egyptian river god Nile looking out over the square from its pedestal. Farther down the Spaccanapoli is the tiny church of **San Nicola a Nilo**, whose horseshoe-shape steps do double duty as an antiques stand. Just across the street, at Via San Biagio dei Librai 114, is the **Monte di Pietà** (open Saturday 9–2), a charitable institution set up five centuries ago. In its **Cappella della Pietà** and opulent 17th-century salons, just beyond the courtyard, there are concerts in summer. Follow the Spacca past Via Duomo to the church of **Pio Monte della Misericordia**, which contains one of the greatest 17th-century altarpieces in Europe, Caravaggio's *The Seven Acts of Mercy*. Because the church is rarely open, stop in the porter's office (in the alley on your left as you face the church) to request permission to view the work (a tip is appropriate). Go back to Via Duomo and turn right to reach the **Duomo**, the majestic cathedral built for Charles I of Anjou in the 14th century. Its centerpiece is the 17th-century chapel of **San Gennaro**, site of the May and September San Gennaro celebrations. Go back onto the Via Duomo and head south a half block until you come to the Via dei Tribunali, another historic thoroughfare lined with imposing churches, among them the elegant **Girolamini** and, at the corner of Via San Gregorio Armeno, the powerful **San Lorenzo Maggiore**. Via San Gregorio Armeno, one of Naples's loveliest streets, is famed for the Rococo splendor of the church of San Gregorio Armeno, whose campanile arches over the street, but you'll also find nearly a dozen presepi stores and stalls, which sell handcrafted figurines and crèches. Back on the Via dei Tribunali, continue your walk east for about 10 blocks to the **Piazza Bellini**, where you can stop for a restorative timeout at a café.

Note that most major churches are open Monday through Saturday from approximately 8 AM (or earlier) to 12:45 PM and again from 4:15 until 7. Sunday hours are generally 7 AM through 1 PM. Many smaller churches do the same; others have sporadic schedules. If a church is closed, the caretaker will often let you in (a small contribution is appreciated).

LODGING OPTIONS:

Albergo Sansevero: Under the same ownership as the Soggiorno Sansevero (see below), this establishment is on one of Spacca's prettiest squares, Piazza Bellini, some 10 blocks from its sister. Rates are higher but include breakfast, and all 11 rooms have private bath. Via S. Maria di Constantinopoli 101, 80138 Napoli, tel. 081/210907, fax 081/211698. Doubles 140,000—150,000 lire. **Grand Hotel Parker's:** Set near the top of the Vomero hill, this exquisitely renovated 19th-century hotel with 73 rooms is the choice of visiting dignitaries. If your quarters don't have a Bay of Naples vista, catch the view from the rooftop restaurant. Corso Vittorio Emanuele 135, 80121 Napoli, tel. 081/761—2474, fax 081/663527, www.bcedit.it/parkers/html. Doubles 390,000 lire, suites 800,000—1,500,000 lire. **Hotel Miramare:** This 31-room hotel is prized for its intimacy, and its waterfront vistas of Mt. Vesuvius, and its central location, just 6 blocks from the Piazza del Plebiscito in the center of Naples. The powerful air-conditioning is a treasure, and owner Enzo Rosolino is one of the warmest, kindest hosts around. Via Nazario Sauro 24, 80132 Napoli, tel. 081/764—7589, fax 081/764—0755, www.hotelmiramare.com. Doubles 350,000—450,000 lire. **Hotel Santa Lucia:** This luxurious place, with 95 rooms and 12 suites, is splendidly located opposite the Borgo Marinaro, the tiny fishermen's marina, on a gracious curve of the Bay of Naples. Hundreds of boats bob in the harbor, which is lined with charming seafood restaurants and dwarfed by the medieval Castel dell'Ovo. Via Partenope 46, 80121 Napoli, tel. 081/764—0666, fax 081/764—8580. Doubles 250,000—320,000 lire, suites from 380,000 lire. **Soggiorno Sansevero:** This unique pension in the heart of Spaccanapoli occupies the former palace of the Princes di Sangro di San Severo, who built the famous family chapel behind the building. Although the palazzo overlooks the opera-set Piazza San Domenico, the Soggiorno is on the palazzo's quiet inner courtyard. The half-dozen rooms are simple, with linoleum floors, modern beds, and great-grandmama's boudoir bureau. They may even come with ghosts: famous composer Carlo Gesualdo, inventor of the madrigal song, murdered his wife and her lover on the premises on October 16, 1590. Piazza S. Domenico Maggiore 9 (Palazzo Sansevero), 80138 Napoli, tel. 081/551—5949, fax 081/211698. Doubles 80,000—130,000 lire.

P O S I T A N O *(7F)*

People head for this most popular of Amalfi Coast destinations, which is set in a natural amphitheater, as though to a hit play. The show does not disappoint. The Moorish-style houses, which seem to be playing leapfrog up Monte Commune and Monte St. Angelo, are prettily painted in every hue (to help returning fishermen spot their home even before unloading their catch).

Through the first half of the 20th century, artists had Positano all to themselves. But in 1953 John Steinbeck let the fish out of the net with a glowing essay in *Harper's Bazaar*. By the 1970s, many fishermen had hung up their nets, making way for a style of life that appealed to Hollywood heavyweights. These days, the freshest catches of the day are the loads of daytrippers arriving on hydrofoils from Capri and Amalfi. Yet, while the town is swamped with them, nothing can ever completely ruin Positano. It's just too beautiful.

DISTANCES 35 miles southeast of Naples, 10 miles east of Sorrento.

GETTING THERE Positano is a popular stop on the bus route along the Amalfi Drive; SITA buses depart frequently from Sorrento and Amalfi. You can also arrive by water, via the Alilauro and Cooperativa Sant'Andrea hydrofoils from Amalfi, Capri, and Sorrento. Cars take the Amalfi Drive (Route 145, which becomes Route 163 near Positano).

WHEN TO GO Cooled by sea breezes and sheltered by the Lattari mountains, Positano enjoys fine weather throughout the year, so you can visit in almost any season. In fact, even December can be magical: Yule trees are fashioned from bougainvillea, orchestra and choir concerts pop up all over town, and a living crèche is enacted for the holidays in neighboring Montepertuso. Positano greets the new year with a big community dance, fireworks on the main beach, and folkloric and musical events. In early June, for the Moda Mare fashion show, there are concerts on the beach and in Nocelle—the sky-high village that looks down on the resort. The first week in September sees the Premi "Leonide Massine" dance and the Vittoria de Sica Film Festival, while the last week of the month brings the Festa del Pesce (fish festival); acrobats and musicians perform in the streets during Montepertuso for Artisti di Strada, also in September. Fireworks mark the main religious festivals, St. Peter's Day on June 29 and the Feast of the Assumption on August 15.

WHAT TO SEE Positano's role is to simply look enchanting, and that it does perfectly. Start your wandering with a stroll to the center of town. If you are coming from the Amalfi Drive bus, get off at the Sponda lower town stop on Via Cristoforo Colombo. Following it downhill, you will pass the glittering **Hotel Le Sirenuse**, turnoffs for many stepped **pathways**, dozens of **boutiques**, and the majestic 18th-century **Palazzo Murat**—be sure to explore its courtyard, Positano's prettiest garden. Follow the crowds a few more steps to the piazza in front of the church of **Santa Maria Assunta**, whose majolica dome is the town's most famous landmark. Continue down to the **Spiaggia Grande**, the town's main beach. A bevy of pretty restaurants beckon here; head instead to the stone pier that's to the far right end of the beach as you face the water; there a staircase climbs up to the Via Positanesi d'America, the loveliest of all the stone pathways in this

lovely town. Past the Trasita Tower you'll find **Lo Guarracino**, an impossibly pretty restaurant with an arbor-like setting over the bay. Feast here on fish, accompanied by a Positano specialty, beer sweetened with Grand Marnier, then continue along the Via Positanesi d'America to the **Fornillo beach**. The sun sets early in Positano; the steep mountainsides block the late afternoon rays. Before it disappears, return to the **Piazza dei Mulini**, where you can catch the local bus (it makes a loop every 30 minutes; buy tickets on board) to travel up to the perchiest parts of town: the **Positano Belvedere** near the Hotel Le Agavi (get off near the Church of Santa Maria delle Grazie) or the historic **cemetery** area, a wonderfully tranquil landmark halfway up the mountain. From these heights, beach level appears hours away. But go down on foot anyway, via one of the famous *scalinatella*, the staircases that zigzag up and down the steep hillsides. With gravity propelling you, you'll reach sea-level in a swift quarter hour, maybe less.

FOR DETAILS The tourist information office is at Via del Saraceno 4, tel. 089/875067. The restaurant Lo Guarracino is at Via Positanesi d'America 12 (tel. 089/875794),

HIKING TO NOCELLE (7F)

La Dolce Vista, p. 20

With its steep streets and staircases, Positano might be the best triathalon training ground in the world. However, even greater cardiovascular challenges await those who make the hike between the hamlets of **Montepertuso** and Nocelle, set in the mountain chain of **St. Angelo a Tre Pizzi**, high above the resort town. To get to Montepertuso (which itself is fairly nondescript), catch the bus leaving every two hours from Positano's central Piazza dei Mulini. After lunch at Montepertuso's roadside café, head out along the only road to Nocelle. After passing the town's famous **natural arch** high on the hillside above you (it is said to have been created by a contest between the Madonna and the Devil, an event celebrated with festivities every July 2), the road continues around the top of a cliff, with the valley leading to the sea far below; the road ends at a stone pathway, which wriggles along clifftops to Nocelle, about half an hour away. From Nocelle, many hiking trails lead back to Positano or upward into the mountains and the *Sentiero degli Dei* (Pathway of the Gods).

BASICS For more walks and detailed information on other area trails, see Julian Tippet's *Landscapes of Sorrento and the Amalfi Coast* (Sunflower Press, London, 1996), which you can find at bookstores and some newsstands in Amalfi, Positano, and Sorrento.

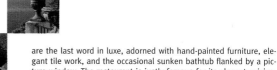

HOTELS LA FENICE AND PALAZZO MURAT

A Tale of Two Positanos, p. 8

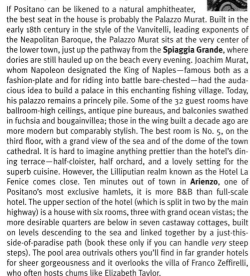

If Positano can be likened to a natural amphitheater, the best seat in the house is probably the Palazzo Murat. Built in the early 18th century in the style of the Vanvitelli, leading exponents of the Neapolitan Baroque, the Palazzo Murat sits at the very center of the lower town, just up the pathway from the **Spiaggia Grande**, where dories are still hauled up on the beach every evening. Joachim Murat, whom Napoleon designated the King of Naples—famous both as a fashion-plate and for riding into battle bare-chested—had the audacious idea to build a palace in this enchanting fishing village. Today, his palazzo remains a princely pile. Some of the 32 guest rooms have ballroom-high ceilings, antique pine bureaus, and balconies swathed in fuchsia and bougainvillea; those in the wing built a decade ago are more modern but comparably stylish. The best room is No. 5, on the third floor, with a grand view of the sea and of the dome of the town cathedral. It is hard to imagine anything prettier than the hotel's dining terrace—half-cloister, half orchard, and a lovely setting for the superb cuisine. However, the Lilliputian realm known as the Hotel La Fenice comes close. Ten minutes out of town in **Arienzo**, one of Positano's most exclusive hamlets, it is more B&B than full-scale hotel. The upper section of the hotel (which is split in two by the main highway) is a house with six rooms, three with grand ocean vistas; the more desirable quarters are below in seven castaway cottages, built on levels descending to the sea and linked together by a just-this-side-of-paradise path (book these only if you can handle *very* steep steps). The pool area outrivals others you'll find in far grander hotels for sheer gorgeousness and it overlooks the villa of Franco Zeffirelli, who often hosts chums like Elizabeth Taylor.

BASICS Hotel Palazzo Murat: Via dei Mulini 23, 84017 Positano (SA), tel. 089/875177, fax 089/811419, www.starnet.it/murat. Doubles 320,000—500,000 lire. Closed Jan—Mar. **Hotel La Fenice:** Via Marconi 4, 84017 Positano (SA), tel. 089/875513, fax 089/811309. Doubles 190,000 lire. No credit cards.

HOTEL SAN PIETRO

The Lush Life, p. 44

With a tiny 17th-century chapel at its entrance honoring Saint Peter, this hotel is a bit of a miracle itself: Dynamited out of sheer rock and set hundreds of feet over the Bay of Positano, it has been considered the architectural wonder of the Amalfi Coast ever since it opened in 1973. The hotel's seclusion, 2 miles south of Positano, is one reason it has long been prized by VIPs. Not so long ago, Hollywood's Julia Roberts confided that for once she was grateful to the paparazzi, for without their nipping at her heels on Capri she would never have sought out the San Pietro. Throughout the hotel, floor-to-ceiling windows bring the outdoors inside, and the 60 guest rooms and suites are the last word in luxe, adorned with hand-painted furniture, elegant tile work, and the occasional sunken bathtub flanked by a picture window. The restaurant is justly famous for its elegant cuisine. Some may find the San Pietro pretty to the point of giddiness, but for others there is simply no place else to stay.

BASICS Via Laurito, 84017 Positano (SA), tel. 089/875455, fax 089/811449, e-mail spietro@stranet.it, www.relaischateaux.fr/san-pietro. Doubles 650,000—740,000 lire, suites 900,000—1,250,000 lire. Closed Nov.—Mar.

LI GALLI ISLANDS (6G)

The Sirens' Call, p. 66

Local folks have nicknamed the rocky archipelago off Positano *Li Galli* (the roosters) because of the islets' resemblance to pecking birds. They have also been known as the home of the legendary Sirens since the days of ancient Greece. The archipelago became the fiefdom in medieval times of French kings, who constructed its lookout tower to ward off pirates. In the 1930s, the Russian choreographer Leonide Massine built a ballet studio on **La Castellucia**, the site of a Roman villa, where some six decades later Rudolf Nureyev spent his last years. During the interim, Li Galli had been the property of the noble Sersale family, who transformed their Positano palazzo into Le Sirenuse in 1951. Today, it is the town's most elegant hotel, with 62 chic rooms and suites: Its public salons glitter with Venetian and Neapolitan antiques; its dining room, festooned with vines and ivy from garden terraces, is extremely fine and spectacularly expensive; and its pool terrace remains *the* place to have lunch in Positano. The hotel yacht takes guests out to Li Galli and other coastal destinations several times a week. Or you can go out with **L'Uomo e il Mare**, the boat-charter operation run by Gennaro Capraro. Some people may consider his 30-foot-long dory rustic and bare bones, but Capraro is delightfully colorful—who else would tell you that Nureyev liked to shock boating parties by jet-skiing past wearing nothing but sea foam? Gennaro's trip to Li Galli takes a day and includes a stop for lunch in the nearby town of **Nerano** (5G); there are usually about nine people aboard. Make your arrangements at the company's office on the **Spiaggia Grande** quay, where you'll often find his friendly, English wife, Valeria.

BASICS Hotel Le Sirenuse: Via C. Colombo 30, 84010 Positano (SA), tel. 089/875066, fax 089/811798, www.sirenuse.it. Doubles 650,000—850,000 lire, suites 1,100,000 lire. **L'Uomo e il Mare:** Gennaro Capraro, Spiaggia Grande Quay, tel. 089/875211 or 875475. Li Galli trip 150,000 lire per person.

R A V E L L O *(F9)*

Ravello is one of the wonders of the world—not for its fine Romanesque churches, or for its spectacular gardens, but for its vistas, which are among the most sublime in Italy. The town arose in the 13th century as a retreat for wealthy families from nearby Amalfi, whose elevated social status was equalled by Ravello's location 1,500 feet atop Monte Cerreto. In the Middle Ages, the Ravellesi grew considerably richer through trade with Saracens; this exchange of cultures resulted in the exquisite Villa Rufolo, one of the most important monuments of Arab-Sicilian architecture. Because of Ravello's secluded setting, its medieval structures remained practically untouched until the 19th century, when a stream of aristocratic Englishmen woke up this sleeping beauty of a town. Before long, D. H. Lawrence, E. M. Forster, and Virginia Woolf were venturing here in search of peace. Even today, Ravello is still so serenely quiet you can mistake it for a monastery—that is, except during the many religious processions, which are usually accompanied by an impromptu Philharmonic of local musicians, and during its world-famous music festival, the Fèstival Musicale di Ravello.

DISTANCES 41 miles southeast of Naples, 18 miles west of Salerno.

GETTING THERE SITA buses terminate in Amalfi; you then transfer for local buses, which depart for Ravello hourly between 7AM and 10PM from the bus stop in Amalfi on the waterfront at Piazza Flavio Gioia. Use of cars is restricted in Ravello; you can park your vehicle for the duration of your stay near the main piazza.

WHEN TO GO To truly enjoy Ravello's unique serenity, visit in early May or late September; spring is the must if you are interested in Amalfi horticulture and the floral displays at the Rufolo and Cimbrone villas. And no longer must you arrive in summer to enjoy the Fèstival Musicale di Ravello: In addition to the Wagner concerts in July and August's *Concerti di Mezzanotte* (midnight concerts, which actually begin at 11 PM) there are many concerts April through November, and even later. The most unusual event is the *Concerto all'Alba,* when the entire town wakes up at 4:30 AM to watch the sun rise over the bay to the accompaniment of music from a full symphony orchestra; this spectacular concert is usually scheduled for the second week of August. Among the many religious festivals held here, the most beautiful is for the Pentecost, usually the first week of June, when geometric designs made of flowers carpet parts of the piazza.

WHAT TO SEE A vista spanning the entire Salernian shore makes Ravello's *fermata* the Miss Universe of bus stops. Nearby, follow the street that tunnels through a hillside to the **Piazza Duomo**, Ravello's café-filled main square, where many townspeople congregate after work and before dinner, during the *passeggiata*. The **Duomo** itself has several medieval treasures, including bronze doors sculpted by Barisano da Trani and a mosaic-encrusted pulpit; other artworks are housed in the small museum below the church. Also in the piazza is the **Bric-a-Brac shop**, a great resource for books on Ravello. Opposite the Duomo is the **Villa Rufolo** (*see below*), famed for its gardens and annual **music festival**. For a closer look at Ravello's most picturesque church, the **Santissima Annunziata**, now a conference center, exit the Villa Rufolo, make a sharp right, and head to the Via dell'Annunziata stairpath, a dizzying descent. To return to the piazza, the scenic Via della Repubblica is the more gentle way back. Back on the piazza, take the Via Richard Wagner, behind the tourist office, to Via San Giovanni del Toro, the address of Ravello's grandest palazzi which are now transformed into hotels. Stop at the **Hotel Caruso Belvedere** for lunch or pack a picnic to enjoy at an adjacent lookout point, the **Belvedere Principessa di Piemonte**. Up the street is the 11th-century church of **San Giovanni del Toro**. After visiting it, backtrack to the piazza and embark on the hilly 10-minute walk along the Via San Francesco to the **Villa Cimbrone**, which seem to be closer to the sky than the sea.

LODGING OPTIONS

There are many options in addition to the celebrated hotels described below. **Palazzo Sasso:** Virgin Airlines' Richard Branson has given one of Ravello's historic palazzi a glitzy makeover: rooftop Jacuzzi, roaring waterfall, Empire-style salons, glass elevator, a gilt-edged restaurant, and 43 opulent rooms and suites. Traditionalists might raise an eyebrow, but even they should adore the extraordinarily comfortable beds, fabulous air-conditioning, and the bathrooms, whose faucets immediately—and miraculously—dispense hot water at the flick of a wrist. Via San Giovanni del Toro 28, 84010 Ravello (SA), tel. 089/818181, fax 089/858900, www.palazzosasso.com. Doubles 550,000—750,000 lire, suites 1,000,000—1,400,000 lire. Closed Jan.—Feb. **Villa Amore:** Modest and friendly, it offers the same matchless views as Ravello's grandest hotels, but the 20 rooms go for a fraction of the price. Via dei Fusco, 84010 Ravello (SA), tel. and fax 089/857135. Doubles 110,000 lire.

FOR DETAILS The Azienda Soggiorno e Turismo di Ravello is at Piazza del Duomo 10 (tel. 089/857096), to your left as you face the 11th-century Duomo stairs. For information on SITA buses, call 081/593—4644.

HOTEL CARUSO BELVEDERE
Inspiration's Realm, p. 14

As aristocratic as a lace-bedecked *contessa*, the Hotel Caruso Belvedere fairly purrs with graciousness and civility. The two dozen rooms and suites are comfortable and simply furnished, but most have *that view* over the Gulf of Salerno. In any event, guests follow in the footsteps of their celebrity predecessors—Arturo Toscanini, King Farouk of Egypt, Margot Fonteyn, Humphrey Bogart, Rosalind Russell—and spend hours in the gardens or enjoying the splendor of the hotel's great salon. Both the kitchen and the hotel's own wine are award-winners. A location across the way from the 14th-century church of **San Giovanni del Toro** makes the Caruso Belvedere one of Italy's most popular venues for weddings, but whatever reason brings you here, a stay at this extraordinary hotel is one of the major joys of a visit to Ravello. The hotel will be closed for renovation for several months in early 2000.

BASICS Via San Giovanni del Toro, 84010 Ravello (SA), tel. 089/857111, fax 857372. Doubles 280,000—360,000 lire, suites 440,000 lire.

VILLA CIMBRONE

Garbo's Shangri-La, p. 52

Called Cimbronium by the ancient Romans, the outcrop of Cimbrone sprang to life in 1904, when Lord Grimthorpe arrived in Ravello needing to wind down after designing the clockworks of London's Big Ben. His idea of relaxation was to build a castle-cum-palazzo in homage to Richard Wagner's trip to Ravello. No doubt having been frustrated by the creative constraints of building a monument emblematic of a world power, as England was when Big Ben ticked its first tock, he added as many architectural furbelows as he could: a turreted tower, a Gothic crypt, and a Norman-Arabic cloister. He surrounded it with magnificent **rose gardens** and added a **Temple of Bacchus, a Grotto of Eve**, and the **Belvedere of Infinity**, which the poet Gabriele d'Annunzio declared the only place in the world you can be "kissed by eternity." Today, Lord Grimthorpe's fancy, transformed into the Hotel Villa Cimbrone by the Vuilleumeier family, could not be more enchanting. The antiques of the Viscountess Frost (Lord Grimthorpe's daughter), rare books, and Vietri faience lend a cozy air to the 14 guest rooms; one of the five suites has magnificent frescoed ceilings. You can satisfy your want to be alone in the room that Greta Garbo once occupied, or ask for the **Peony Room**, one of the few with a private balcony over the bay. The catch is that the villa can only be visited inside if you're staying there (otherwise, you can see just the gardens, crypt, and cloister). And it can't be reached by car—getting there requires a brisk 15-minute hike from Ravello's center. Not to worry: Porters will carry your luggage, and the distance keeps things unforgettably peaceful.

BASICS Villa Cimbrone and Hotel Villa Cimbrone: Via Santa Chiara 26, 84010 Ravello (SA), tel. 089/857459, fax 089/857777. Open daily 10—sunset. Admission for gardens, crypt, and cloister 5,000 lire. Doubles 400,000—475,000 lire, suites 550,000—600,000 lire. Closed Nov.—Mar.

VILLA RUFOLO

The Bluest View in the World, p. 36

The 13th-century Villa Rufolo was the creation of Landolfo Rufolo, a banker so rich he held the crown of Charles of Anjou in pawn. After Sir Francis Nevil Reid, a Scotsman, acquired the villa in 1851, he hired Michele Ruggiero, head of the excavations at Pompeii, to do a total restoration. When work was complete, the terrace gardens had been bedded out with rare cycads, cordylines, and palms in the manner of a Victorian parterre; in her book, *In My Tower* (1898), Lady Paget called the result the most romantic sight she had ever seen. The villa, which you enter from Ravello's main square, is famed for its assemblage of Italian, Norman, and Saracenic architecture. Highlights are the **Moorish Cloister**—an Arab-Sicilian delight with interlacing lancet arcs and polychromatic palmette decoration—and the 14th-century **Torre Maggiore**, renamed Klingsor's Tower in honor of Richard Wagner's landmark 1880 visit, a charming spot for chamber-music recitals (except in rainy weather, when concerts take place in a charmless room nearby). Beyond the tower lie the incomparable **terrace gardens**, whose lower level hosts the main orchestral **concerts** of the Ravello's music festival. Other festival performances, including the midnight concerts and the dawn concert (both in August), are also held here, as are many other musical events throughout the year.

BASICS Piazza Vescovado, 84010 Ravello (SA), tel. 089/857866. Daily 9AM—sunset. Admission 4,000 lire. Most evening concerts begin at 9:30 PM; others begin at 6:30 or 11 PM. For schedules and specific prices, contact the Fèstival Musicale di Ravello, Ravello Concert Society, 84010 Ravello, tel. 089/858149, fax 089/857977, e-mail info@rcs.amalficoast.it.

SORRENTO *(F5)*

The great 19th-century French novelist Stendhal called Sorrento "the most beautiful place on earth," and in many ways it still is, not least in thanks to its spectacular location. Surrounded by orange and lemon groves and perched high on a bluff on the peninsula created by the Lattari mountains, it has a stunning view of Mt. Vesuvius and the Bay of Naples. When literati sang its praises in the Grand Tour era, palatial hotels went up to accommodate the titled lords and ladies who rushed to visit. The English, especially, left their stamp on the city, which is still notably civil and genteel: You'll find afternoon cocktails and thé dansants in the deluxe hotels; you don't have to lock your car; and if you leave your wallet in a phone booth, you can reasonably expect it to be there when you return. There are no major tourist attractions; the city itself—with its enchanting sherbet-hued palazzi, its bouquets of villas, and its gaily striped awnings and serenading waiters—is the draw.

DISTANCES 31 miles south of Naples.

GETTING THERE Without a car the best way to get from Naples to Sorrento is via the Ferrovia Circumvesuviana train, which departs frequently from Naples's Stazione Centrale. The trip takes about an hour; the 20 stops en route include Herculaneum (4C) and Pompeii (7D). Another way to make the trip is via the Alilaura and Caremar hydrofoils, which pull up at Sorrento's Piccola Marina. (Here, you can also get ferries for Ischia, Amalfi, and Capri.) By car from Naples, head south on Route 18, then cut west at the junction with Route 145. From Sorrento's Circumvesuviana station, SITA buses provide frequent service to and from other towns on the Amalfi Coast. In Sorrento, for tickets, stop at the newsstand in the station; between noon and 4, when the newsstand is usually closed, get them at the Mayflower Bar or the Bar dei Fiori at the Parco Lauro a block south of the station. If you are planning to get around the area by bus, it's a good idea to load up on tickets when you have the chance.

WHEN TO GO The soft Sorrentine sunlight seems nearly constant from mid-February until mid-November. In the 19th-century, it was the fashion to arrive in spring, in time to see and smell the lemon and orange blossoms. If you can't make it then, try for early fall, since the city is overrun in July and August. Still, summer is the season for cultural activities: There are performances of the Spettacoli Teatrali (a summer theater), and concerts in the Chiostro del Paradiso (Paradise Cloister) at the Chiesa di San Francesco from June to September, and classical music concerts at the Cocumella Church between May and September; the Festa di Sant'Anna, with fireworks at the Marina Grande, is on July 26.

WHAT TO SEE When you leave the Stazione Centrale, a 10-minute walk to your left along the Corso Italia brings you to the café-filled **Piazza Tasso**, the center of historic Sorrento. The Via S. Cesareo is the major artery off the southern end of the piazza near the Victorian clock tower, you enter a labyrinth of alleys and streets lined with charming boutiques; it leads you to a tiny square and the 16th-century **Sedile Dominova**, a lavishly frescoed loggia that was once an assembly hall for town nobles. (At night it is beautifully illuminated, so you must—repeat, must—return here to feast your eyes on it and to experience the joyous **Caffè 2000**, whose umbrella tables are filled with delighted tourists singing along with the caffè band's "O Sole Mio.") From the Sedile you can easily spot the wedding-cake campanile of the town **Duomo** at the end of Via Giuliani. Inside the church are some impressive examples of local *intarsi* (marquetry). Backtrack along the Via Giuliani until you reach the Via Veneto, and turn right to the **Chiesa di San Francesco**, with its famous **Chiostro del Paradiso**. Just beyond this point lies the belvedere of the **Villa Communale**, whose prize is a Cinerama view of the Bay of Naples. Back on the Via Veneto, turn right

and head to the **Piazza Vittoria** to view one of Sorrento's most picturesque buildings, the home of 16th-century writer Torquato Tasso; steps away, across the small square, enjoy a time-out at the balcony café of the **Hotel Bellevue Syrene**. From there, continue south along Via Marina Grande, past the Villa Astor (private) to the **Marina Grande**, the town's fishing port. For the return trip, you can hop on a bus, or backtrack on Via Veneto and Via S. Francesco to the quaint **Piazza S. Antonio**. Off this piazza on the Via Luigi de Maio (to your left as you enter the piazza) is the grand house that the local tourist office shares with the **Circolo dei Forestieri**, a popular meeting place for travelers with a vast terrace bar that's pleasant for drinks. Or, for an even more Sorrentine send-off to your day, stop off at the **Albergo Lorelei et Londres**. To get there, head back to Piazza Tasso; pop into Via Pietà on the southeast corner of the piazza to see the **Palazzo Correale's** lovely **Majolica Courtyard**, which dates from 1772; then, back on the piazza, find the Via Correale and walk north. At the **Museo Correale**, turn left on Via Califano, which leads to the Albergo, a turn-of-the-century hotel that distills all the beauty of Sorrento into one exquisite composition. Toast the setting sun from its lovely terrace-café.

FOR DETAILS The Azienda di Soggiorno Cura e Turismo di Sant'Agnello e Sorrento is at Via Luigi de Maio 35, tel. 081/807—4033. For bus information, contact SITA in Naples, tel. 081/593—4644.

ALBERGO LORELEI ET LONDRES
What Lucy Missed, p. 16

As if forgotten by time, the Albergo Lorelei et Londres looks like a vintage travel poster; this astonishing relic conjures up turn-of-the-century Sorrento better than any other hotel in town. With its red awnings and tablecloths, its terrace restaurant is one of the most enchanting settings in all of Italy. So even if you don't stay here, at least opt for lunch, an afternoon drink, or dinner in its inexpensive restaurant. Upstairs, beyond the welcoming lobby adorned with fading photographs and plants, the 23 guest rooms are slightly tatterdemalion, with little historic flavor—but who cares when **Mt. Vesuvius** is posing just outside the window. Book a room facing the bay and try to avoid the two rooms that open onto the street. And hurry, before the 21st century spoils this treasure.

BASICS Via Califano 2, 80067 Sorrento (NA), tel. and fax 81/807—3187. Doubles 130,000 lire including breakfast and dinner.

HOTEL EXCELSIOR VITTORIA
A Little Romance, p. 40

Still a regal realm, the Excelsior Vittoria became the favored sanctuary of the king of Siam, the emperor of Austria-Hungary, and the maharajah of Indore practically the moment it opened its doors in 1834.

Comprised of three Belle Epoque chalets, this 93-room hotel is hidden within a lush garden park, apart from the rolling **Piazza Tasso**, directly outside. The interiors are a monument to the Grand Tour sensibility. Public salons are arrayed with decorative *objets*, corridors feel like dream sequences from a Visconti movie, and the grandest guest quarters (including one that sheltered both Enrico Caruso and Luciano Pavarotti) wear an operatic opulence; the better rooms have lovely voile curtains from England, antique iron beds, and frescoed vaults and moldings. The dining room is Sorrento's most gilded, and as the kitchen continues to improve, crowds gather on Sunday evenings, drawn for a buffet and dancing on a terrace teetering over the Bay of Naples.

BASICS Piazza Tasso 34, 80067 Sorrento (NA), tel. 081/807—1044, fax 081/877—1206, www.exwitt.it. Doubles 480,000—619,000 lire, suites 800,000—2,000,000 lire.

VILLA POMPEIANA

What Lord Astor Knew, p. 48

Lucullus, legendary for his banquets during ancient Roman times, would have given a thumbs-up to the Villa Pompeiana, Lord Astor's lavish recreation of Pompeii's most famous villa, the House of the Vetti Brothers, now the restaurant of the 72-room Bellevue Syrene, one of Italy's most historic hotels and a bastion of Sorrento at its most *soigné*. At dinnertime, settle into a feast of the restaurant's signature *paffutelli della Syrene* (ravioli stuffed with *caciotta*, ricotta and Parmesan cheeses), Li Galli lobster, and oranges in Limoncello liqueur. Or come for a light lunch, tea, or an apéritif on the adjoining *terrazzo all'antica*—the grandest terrace between Rome and Cecil B. DeMille. Then, if you're a lucky guest at the Bellevue Syrene, you can retire to your room. Lucky is the operative word: The service is unimaginably cordial, the decor the ultimate in richness—glowing chandeliers, Louis-Phillipe rugs, 19th-century murals painted by the Fluss brothers (imported from Vienna to make King Ludwig of Bavaria feel at home). The private beach is directly below the hotel.

BASICS Piazza della Vittoria 5, 80067 Sorrento (NA), tel. 081/878—1024, fax 081/878—3963, www.bellevue@syrene.it. Doubles 440,000 lire, suites 550,000 lire.

NEAR SORRENTO
SANT'AGATA, SANT'AGNELLO, TORRE ANNUNZIATA

The Sorrentine peninsula juts out from the Apennine mountains into the Bay of Naples, and extends from the foothills of Mt. Vesuvius to the Punta Campanella (4H), itself only a few miles from the isle of Capri just across the bay. Although the city of Sorrento is the penin-

sula's largest, most glowing jewel, you will also find Sant'Agata sui Due Golfi (5G), famed for its panoramic view and for the restaurant Don Alfonso 1800; the clifftop hamlet of Sant'Agnello (5F), home to two of Italy's prettiest hotels; and, five minutes away from crowded Pompeii (7D), the town of Torre Annunziata (6D)—modern and dreary but also the site of the ancient Villa Poppaea.

DON ALFONSO 1800, SANT'AGATA SUI DUE GOLFI (5G)

Feasting Under the Sun, p. 26

Members of Monaco's reigning family, passionate food lovers from around the world, and the Michelin judges who made Don Alfonso 1800 one of only two three-star restaurants in Italy several years ago, are just a few of the fans of master chef Alfonso Iaccarino who, in 1973, created southern Italy's foremost culinary shrine out of what had once been his father's pizzeria in a Sant'Agata inn. Mediterranean modern is the Iaccarino credo, and every dish is based on the freshest of seasonal ingredients and delicacies, whether shrimp from the Bay of Naples or pheasant from Scotland. The menu is studded with wonders like mousse di prosciutto di Parma, quail *dal viaggio in Birmania,* and soufflé di Nirvana. Alfonso's enchanting wife, Livia, circulates through the dining area, distributing her own spectacularly welcoming smiles. Wine lovers should plead for a tour of the legendary wine cellar, in an Oscan king's tomb deep within the mountain, perhaps to ogle a Roman amphora dating from 30 BC. Above the restaurant are three apartments, part of the Relais & Chateaux chain. (Light sleepers beware: Don Alfonso is on the main square of Sant'Agata, adjacent to the 17th-century church of **S. Maria delle Grazie**, whose bells toll every quarter hour around the clock.) A 30-minute hike to the medieval **Monastero Il Deserto**, whose belvedere offers a grand vista of the two bays, could serve as a natural pre-dinner apéritif.

GETTING THERE Cresting a mountain 1,300 feet above the Bay of Naples, Sant' Agata sui Due Golfi can easily be reached via local bus from the Circumvesuviana Station in the center of Sorrento.

BASICS Piazza Sant'Agata 11, 80064 Sant'Agata sui Due Golfi (NA), tel. and fax 081/878—0026. Doubles 270,000 lire. Closed Mon.—Tues. Oct.—May, Mon. June—Sept., and mid-Jan.—Feb.

THE PARCO DEI PRINCIPI, SANT'AGNELLO (5F)

The Secret Garden, p. 78

Once the suburb of choice for Sorrento, Sant'Agnello remains a beautiful spot along the Bay of Naples, still offering a taste of the aristocratic life at its two famous hotels, the Parco dei Principi and the **Cocumella**. Legendary names—Johann Wolfgang von Goethe, the Duke of Wellington, Hans Christian Andersen, Robert Peel, and Joachim Murat, the king of Naples—put the Cocumella on the map in the early 19th century, and it remains the most luxurious hotel on the Sorrentine peninsula. Many superb architectural features from its days as a 16th-century Jesuit monastery are intact: frescoed ceilings, stained glass windows, a medieval cloister, a 17th-century church. The Del Papa family, which owns the place, has adorned the 60 rooms and suites with antique prints, brocade wallpapers, and fireplaces. The public spaces form a grand enfilade filled with Victorian furniture, the breakfast is one of the most sumptuous in Italy, and there are regular excursions on the Bay of Naples on the *Vera*, a 90-foot yacht dating from the 19th century. The exquisite pool area is set within a century-old park where well-tended paths thread together gardens, lemon groves, and a grand terrace overlooking the bay; an elevator carries guests to a private bathing pier. Next door to the Cocumella is the 190-room Hotel Parco dei Principi, centered in the magnificent 18th-century park created by the Count of Siracusa. The count's cliffside villa is now open only for special events; today's guests stay in a striking, white-on-white hotel designed by Gio Ponti in 1962. A favorite of tour groups, this hotel is generally packed—and it's particularly friendly and festive as a result.

GETTING THERE Sant'Agnello is 2 miles north of Sorrento's historic center, accessible by bus from Sorrento's central Piazza Tasso or via a scenic walk.

WHEN TO GO The special event to note here is the Concerti di Cocumella weekend chamber music concert series, which takes place between May and September at the 17th-century church of Santa Maria, now part of the Grand Hotel Cocumella.

BASICS Grand Hotel Cocumella: Via Cocumella 7, 80065 Sant'Agnello, Sorrento (NA), tel. 081/878—2933, fax 081/878—3786. Doubles 500,000 lire, suites 920,000 lire. Hotel Parco dei Principi: Via Rota 1, 80067 Sant'Agnello, Sorrento (NA), tel. 081/878—4644, fax 081/878—3786. Doubles 400,000 lire, suites 555,000 lire. Concerti dei Cocumella: For information and tickets, call 081/878—2933.

VILLA POPPAEA, OPLONTIS, TORRE ANNUNZIATA (6D)

At Home with an Empress, p. 76

Although Pompeii is near the top of many sightseeing lists, this famous archeological site can be sorely disappointing: By midday the ancient Roman town is often scorched by the sun (don't bother to look for shade, as Vesuvius's first-century fireworks left few houses with roofs) and tour groups jam the rutted streets. For true Roman splendor and a site happily bereft of crowds, visit **Oplontis**, another excavation, and its Villa Poppaea, one stop away from Pompeii on the Circumvesuviana train in the town of Torre Annunziata. This gigantic villa is a veritable palace compared to the houses in Pompeii. Its roof is intact, its grand *viridarium* (garden) is filled with oleander trees, and room after room displays spectacular **murals** in the Second and Third Pompeiian styles (buy the color booklet on sale at the newsstand you pass en route from the train station if you want to know the difference). Almost half the palatial house was given over to servant quarters and kitchens. The emperor Nero married Poppaea—whose patrician family had originally come from Pompeii—in 62 AD, and was so smitten with her that he got rid of his first wife, their son, and his mother, Agrippina, in order to clear the way to the altar. Poppaea was as intelligent as she was extravagant; the philosopher St. Paul was her friend. She died in 65 AD, while pregnant, after Nero kicked her in the abdomen. The villa was soon abandoned, but its artistic style and beautiful colonnades were copied when Nero built his palace in Rome, the Golden House, in 66 AD.

GETTING THERE To get to Oplontis, take the Circumvesuviana train from Sorrento to Torre Annunziata, the stop after Scavi di Pompeii. A three-block walk brings you to the excavated villa.

BASICS Via Sepolcri 1, Torre Annunziata, tel. 081/862—1755. Open daily from 9 AM until an hour before sunset. Admission 4,500 lire.

Author and photographer Robert I.C. Fisher, a Fodor's staff editor, is a romantic to the core and an Italian at heart. His love affair with the Boot began during his graduate studies in Renaissance art history under Sir John Pope-Hennessy at the Institute of Fine Arts, New York City; it was later fueled by research for a *Town & Country* profile of a noted 16th-century Roman palazzo; and it has continued to flourish during his work on several editions of Fodor's Italy guides.